T0320462

Predictive Analysis on Large Data for Actionable Knowledge:

Emerging Research and Opportunities

Muhammad Usman
Shaheed Zulfikar Ali Bhutto Institute of Science and Technology, Pakistan

M. Usman
Pakistan Scientific and Technological Information Center (PASTIC), Pakistan

A volume in the Advances in Data Mining and Database Management (ADMDM) Book Series

Published in the United States of America by
IGI Global
Information Science Reference (an imprint of IGI Global)
701 E. Chocolate Avenue
Hershey PA, USA 17033
Tel: 717-533-8845
Fax: 717-533-8661
E-mail: cust@igi-global.com
Web site: http://www.igi-global.com

Library of Congress Cataloging-in-Publication Data

Names: Usman, Muhammad, 1986- author. | Usman, M., 1982- author.
Title: Predictive analysis on large data for actionable knowledge : emerging
  research and opportunities / by Muhammad Usman and M. Usman.
Description: Hershey, PA : Information Science Reference, [2018] | Includes
  bibliographical references.
Identifiers: LCCN 2017034509| ISBN 9781522550297 (hardcover) | ISBN
  9781522550303 (ebook)
Subjects: LCSH: Data mining. | Big data. | Forecasting--Data processing. |
  Forecasting--Statistical methods.
Classification: LCC QA76.9.D343 U86 2018 | DDC 005.7--dc23 LC record available at https://
lccn.loc.gov/2017034509

This book is published in the IGI Global book series Advances in Data Mining and Database Management (ADMDM) (ISSN: 2327-1981; eISSN: 2327-199X)

British Cataloguing in Publication Data
A Cataloguing in Publication record for this book is available from the British Library.

All work contributed to this book is new, previously-unpublished material.
The views expressed in this book are those of the authors, but not necessarily of the publisher.

For electronic access to this publication, please contact: eresources@igi-global.com.

Advances in Data Mining and Database Management (ADMDM) Book Series

ISSN:2327-1981
EISSN:2327-199X

Editor-in-Chief: David Taniar, Monash University, Australia

MISSION

With the large amounts of information available to organizations in today's digital world, there is a need for continual research surrounding emerging methods and tools for collecting, analyzing, and storing data.

The **Advances in Data Mining & Database Management (ADMDM)** series aims to bring together research in information retrieval, data analysis, data warehousing, and related areas in order to become an ideal resource for those working and studying in these fields. IT professionals, software engineers, academicians and upper-level students will find titles within the ADMDM book series particularly useful for staying up-to-date on emerging research, theories, and applications in the fields of data mining and database management.

COVERAGE

- Decision Support Systems
- Data Mining
- Quantitative Structure–Activity Relationship
- Sequence analysis
- Neural Networks
- Association Rule Learning
- Data Analysis
- Database Security
- Factor Analysis
- Database Testing

IGI Global is currently accepting manuscripts for publication within this series. To submit a proposal for a volume in this series, please contact our Acquisition Editors at Acquisitions@igi-global.com or visit: http://www.igi-global.com/publish/.

Titles in this Series

For a list of additional titles in this series, please visit:
https://www.igi-global.com/book-series/advances-data-mining-database-management/37146

Applications of Finite Markov Chains and Fuzzy Logic in Learning Contexts Emerging ...
Michael Voskoglou (Graduate Technological Educational Institute of Western Greece Greece)
Engineering Science Reference • ©2018 • 193pp • H/C (ISBN: 9781522533283) • US $175.00

Exploring the Convergence of Big Data and the Internet of Things
A.V. Krishna Prasad (K.L. University, India)
Engineering Science Reference • ©2018 • 332pp • H/C (ISBN: 9781522529477) • US $245.00

Deep Learning Innovations and Their Convergence With Big Data
S. Karthik (SNS College of Technology, Anna University, India) Anand Paul (Kyungpook National University, South Korea) and N. Karthikeyan (Mizan-Tepi University, Ethiopia)
Information Science Reference • ©2018 • 265pp • H/C (ISBN: 9781522530152) • US $205.00

Modern Technologies for Big Data Classification and Clustering
Hari Seetha (Vellore Institute of Technology-Andhra Pradesh, India) M. Narasimha Murty (Indian Institute of Science, India) and B. K. Tripathy (VIT University, India)
Information Science Reference • ©2018 • 360pp • H/C (ISBN: 9781522528050) • US $215.00

Data Visualization and Statistical Literacy for Open and Big Data
Theodosia Prodromou (University of New England, Australia)
Information Science Reference • ©2017 • 365pp • H/C (ISBN: 9781522525127) • US $205.00

Web Semantics for Textual and Visual Information Retrieval
Aarti Singh (Guru Nanak Girls College, Yamuna Nagar, India) Nilanjan Dey (Techno India College of Technology, India) Amira S. Ashour (Tanta University, Egypt & Taif University, Saudi Arabia) and V. Santhi (VIT University, India)
Information Science Reference • ©2017 • 290pp • H/C (ISBN: 9781522524830) • US $185.00

For an enitre list of titles in this series, please visit:
https://www.igi-global.com/book-series/advances-data-mining-database-management/37146

701 East Chocolate Avenue, Hershey, PA 17033, USA
Tel: 717-533-8845 x100 • Fax: 717-533-8661
E-Mail: cust@igi-global.com • www.igi-global.com

Table of Contents

Preface.. vi

Chapter 1
Introduction..1

Chapter 2
Literature Review..14

Chapter 3
Conceptual Model for Predictive Analysis on Large Data.....................59

Chapter 4
Experimental Study I: Automobile Dataset 91

Chapter 5
Experimental Study II: Adult Dataset..111

Chapter 6
Experimental Study III: Forest Cover Type Dataset...........................133

Conclusion 151

Related Readings... 155

About the Authors... 175

Index.. 176

Preface

A huge amount of data of different formats is continually being collected from multiple sources. This fast growth in data has highlighted the requirement of developing new tools and techniques that can intelligently assist analysts to discover meaningful and useful knowledge. Data mining and data warehousing are two key technologies for discovering knowledge from large datasets. The combined use of data mining and data warehousing techniques such as Online Analytical Mining (OLAM) has received substantial consideration in academia as well as industry as they are the vital tools used for knowledge discovery. Data mining for knowledge discovery has emerged as a promising discipline in Computer Science in order to automatically extract and predict patterns representing knowledge from large datasets.

Recently, pattern extraction and prediction techniques have been applied independently on large datasets for discovering useful knowledge. However, the literature lacks the presence of integrated techniques which allow pattern extraction and prediction in a single framework. Moreover, the available methodologies for pattern extraction and prediction have number of issues. Firstly, the previously proposed methodologies can only cater for one type of discovery task. These methodologies can either be used to discover cubes of interest or to provide diverse association rules from multidimensional schema. However, there could be cases where analysts have an interest in both types of knowledge discovery tasks. For example, a user may first want to investigate data cube regions and after finding interesting regions, would like to discover the interesting and strong association rules from such dense informative regions. In such cases, there is a strong need to have a generic methodology that facilitates the users with multiple types of discovery tasks.

Secondly, techniques have not been proposed for mining at multiple levels of abstraction, which provide the ability to extract and predict patterns at different levels of data hierarchy. Thirdly, majority of the proposed methodologies in the past do not evaluate the extracted patterns using advanced statistical measures. Finally, the available approaches do not provide an effective visualization support for large number of extracted patterns. To date, a few solutions have been proposed for the aforementioned problems in the literature. Existing methodologies tend to rely on expert users supplying information to guide the discovery process.

In this book, a novel methodology has been proposed which allows the extraction and prediction of patterns at multiple levels of abstraction. For domain knowledge independency, the methodology involves a robust procedure handling both numeric and nominal data at once using a single method. The proposed methodology does not assume that user input is available, but is flexible enough to accommodate such information should it be available. It comprises of two algorithms to automate the multi-dimensional schema generation, and loading of data to this schema in order to remove the manual processing at multiple levels. Moreover, extraction and prediction results are evaluated using advanced statistical measures. Finally, the methodology provides a visualization component which enables the interactive analysis of large number of extracted patterns. The three experimental studies conducted on real word datasets taken from UCI Machine Learning repository revealed that the inclusion of different variable ranking technique results in more informative patterns. The visualization component also provides the ability of interactive analysis of extracted patterns. These results show that methodology enables the extraction of informative and diverse patterns as well as prediction of patterns at multiple levels of abstraction with an interactive analysis support.

The proposed methodology would also be of interest to practitioners as commercial interest in high volume, high dimensional data analysis continues to grow. However, the proposed methodology definitely does not exhaust the challenges of comprehensive and completely automatic analysis for non-conventional domains, but we expect it to be useful for a wide range of application scenarios.

This preface introduces the general context, the aims and the rationale of this book with a brief description of each chapter's contents. The motivation for integrating pattern extraction and pattern prediction using machine learning in non-conventional application domains for improving the knowledge discovery process is given.

AIMS AND OBJECTIVES

The primary objective of this book is to provide insights concerning the integration of pattern extraction and pattern prediction techniques for enhancing the overall knowledge discovery process. This is a front-line and important topic that is of interest in both industry and knowledge engineering research community. The current approaches of knowledge discovery in industry are ad-hoc where pattern extraction and prediction has been dealt separately. There is no standard rule of thumb in integrating these two types of techniques. This book reports on the existing gaps in this area and presents the novel approaches to bridge the existing gaps.

TARGET AUDIENCE AND TOPICS COVERED

The target audience of this book includes decision makers, data analysts, data scientists, Machine learning experts, academicians, researchers, advanced-level students, technology developers, and Business Intelligence (BI) professionals will find this text useful in furthering their research exposure to relevant topics in knowledge discovery and assisting in furthering their own research efforts in this field. Similarly, data analysts from a variety of domains could learn from the three real world case studies that how they can utilize the existing methods for mining useful patterns and predicting future trends accurately.

This book covers the following topics relating to pattern extraction and prediction.

- Data mining techniques: clustering, classification, association rules, decision trees, etc.
- Data and knowledge representation.
- Knowledge discovery framework and process, including pre- and post-processing.
- Integration of data warehousing, OLAP and data mining.
- Exploratory data analysis.
- Interactive data exploration/visualization and discovery.
- Pattern Mining and Prediction.
- Pattern Recognition using diverse datasets, i.e., Automobile, Census and Forest.
- Pattern mining support for designing intelligent information systems.

I hope this book will highlight the need for growth and research in the area of improving knowledge discovery through the integrated use of data mining techniques. This volume consists of seven chapters in total.

Chapter 1, "Introduction," introduces the context in general, the aims and rationale of the book followed by a brief review of the contents of chapters in this book. The motivation for the multi-level pattern extraction and prediction is given, followed by identifying different limitations in existing techniques in this subject to satisfy the requirements of multi-level pattern extraction and prediction.

Chapter 2, "Literature Review," discusses the integrated techniques of knowledge discovery, identify gaps, and draw research objectives of this research. The chapter firstly discusses the pattern extraction techniques from large datasets, for example, a data warehouse, followed by pattern prediction techniques. A review of pattern extraction and prediction is presented on the basis of knowledge independency, multi-level mining ability, advanced evaluation of results and visualization ability. At the end, a summary of issues in the current research are presented followed by the research objectives of this research.

Chapter 3, "Conceptual Model for Predictive Analytics on Large Data," provides an overview of the proposed model for pattern extraction and pattern prediction over data warehouses. The main objective of the research is to provide single model for pattern extraction and prediction. The objectives include an automated way to selection of variables for the mining process, automated schema design, advanced evaluation of extracted patterns and visualization of extracted patterns.

Chapter 4, "Experimental Study I: Automobile Dataset," provides implementation of the proposed model on Automobile data set. The chapter includes the implementation of pattern extraction from this dataset by following a series of steps discussed in the proposed model chapter. It also includes detailed implementation of pattern prediction from Automobile dataset for prediction of numeric variables, nominal variables and aggregate data. The implementation of pattern prediction is also a series of steps.

Chapter 5, "Experimental Study II: Adult Dataset," provides experimental study of the proposed model on Adult data set. The chapter includes the implementation of pattern extraction from this dataset by following a series of steps as discussed before. It also includes detailed implementation of pattern prediction of numeric variables, nominal variables and aggregate data.

Chapter 6, "Experimental Study III: Forest Cover Type Dataset," provides implementation of the proposed model on Forest Cover Type data set. The chapter includes the implementation of pattern extraction from this dataset by following a series of steps discussed in the proposed model chapter. It also includes detailed implementation of pattern prediction from Automobile dataset for prediction of numeric variables, nominal variables and aggregate data.

The Conclusion summarizes the usage of data mining and data warehousing techniques in hybrid fashion for pattern extraction and prediction in large data sets. The particular focus remained on creating domain knowledge independent technique which could work on multiple levels of abstraction, deploys advanced measures of evaluation on extract patterns and has the visualization capability for better understanding of patterns in a graphical interface. The experimental studies on three datasets have shown the potential of this methodology. In this concluding chapter, a summary of the book is presented and future guidelines are discussed.

As an author, I hope this book will provide readers some specific challenge that motivates the development and enhancement of knowledge discovery through the integrated use of data mining techniques. I also hope that this book will serve as an introductory material to the researchers and practitioners interested in this promising area of research.

Muhammad Usman
September 2017

Chapter 1
Introduction

ABSTRACT

This chapter introduces the context in general, the aims, and the rationale of the book. It follows this with a brief review of the contents of chapters in this book. The motivation for the multi-level pattern extraction and prediction is given, followed by identifying different limitations in existing techniques in this subject to satisfy the requirements of multi-level pattern extraction and prediction.

1.1 INTRODUCTION: PATTERN EXTRACTION AND PREDICTION IN LARGE DATASETS

A large volume of data is present in all domains today. Apart from handling the storage of data, researchers have also been interested to use this data for knowledge extraction purposes. Recently, techniques have been adapted to find hidden and interesting patterns from large data sets (Frawley, Piatetsky-Shapiro, & Matheus (1992); Fayyad, Piatetsky-Shapiro, & Smyth (1996); Goebel & Gruenwald, 1999). For knowledge discovery data mining and data warehousing have played a major role independently (Cios, Pedrycz, & Swiniarski, 1998; Wang, 1999; Palpanas, 2000). Data mining has widely been used for knowledge discovery in all domains like business, medicine, education, and science as it aims to extract patterns from large data sets (Han, Kamber, & Chiang, 1997; Hand, Mannila, & Smyth, 2001). On the other hand data warehouses have been used for exploratory analysis by the researchers. Researchers have worked in past for data warehouse evolution in various

DOI: 10.4018/978-1-5225-5029-7.ch001

directions (Kimball & Caserta, 2011; Berson & Smith,1997; Chaudhuri & Dayal, 1997). However recently, researchers have started using both domains in hybrid fashion (You, Dillon, & Liu, 2001; Liu & Guo, 2001; Chen et al, 2006; Hsu & Chien, 2007; Messaoud, Rabaséda, Boussaid, & Missaoui, 2006; Messaoud, Rabaséda, Rokia, & Boussaid, 2007; Usman, Asghar, & Fong, 2009; Korikache & Yahia, 2014). The hybrid techniques are generally used for knowledge discovery and have strengthened the process. Researchers have continued for advancements in this area. The hybrid techniques include pattern prediction and extraction in multidimensional environment.

Han, Pei, and Kamber (2011) have defined different characteristics of a mining processing working in a multidimensional environment. Authors have suggested that mining process needs to be domain independent, so that analysts can use the process without domain knowledge. Secondly, a good mining process provides facilities for mining on different subsets of data and at varying levels of abstraction in a multi-dimensional environment. The extracted knowledge needs to be validated through advanced measures of interestingness as well. Moreover, the process is strengthened by adding a visualization component to the process.

The hybrid techniques discussed above have been used for knowledge discovery in almost all domains in past (Bogdanova & Georgieva, 2005; Yadav & Pal, 2015; McNamara, Crossley, Roscoe, Allen, &and Dai, 2015; Messaoud et al, 2006; Messaoud et al, 2007; Ordonez & Chen 2009; Bodin-Niemczuk, Messaoud, Rabaséda, & Boussaid, 2008). In some cases, it is important for a knowledge discovery to be guided by a domain expert, so techniques have been proposed in past to deal with such cases (Kamber, Han, &Chiang, 1997; Messaoud et al, 2006; Messaoud et al, 2007; Ordonez & Chen, 2009; Kamber et al, 1997; Sarawagi, Agrawal, & Megiddo, 1998). However in most cases, knowledge discovery aims to find hidden and interesting patterns. There are some approaches which mine over data warehouse in automated way (Usman, Pears, & Fong, 2013; Ordonez & Chen, 2009; Azeem, Usman, & Ahmad, 2014).

As discussed above, another important feature of a mining process is the ability to work at multiple levels of abstraction. While mining in a multi-dimensional environment, not many techniques exist which work at multiple levels of abstraction. Few techniques allow pattern extraction from data warehouses with the help of hierarchical clustering (Azeem et al, 2014,

Korikache & Yahia, 2014). Similarly, pattern prediction has also been done at multiple levels with the help of hierarchical clustering. These approaches work at multiple levels of abstraction and have the ability to extract and predict patterns (Zhu, 1998), Wang et al., 2013; Usman et al., 2013). These techniques have shown the potential of hybrid approaches in knowledge discovery at multiple levels.

Apart from the ability to mine at multiple levels, patterns extracted and predicted from a data mining process are normally evaluated at the last stage. Techniques have already been proposed for evaluation of extracted knowledge from data mining processes in past (Han et al., 2011, Kantardzic, 2011) in general. Since the target of hybrid approaches is also to extract knowledge either through pattern prediction techniques or pattern extraction techniques, such knowledge must be validated. Authors have proposed techniques for evaluation purposes in hybrid approaches. Since data mining methods were initially supported for mining over transaction databases, therefore the techniques for evaluation were majorly based on conventional measures like support, confidence, and accuracy. However, while mining in a multidimensional environment, data is available in aggregate form, so authors have proposed measures like Lift, Loevinger, Rae, Con, Hill, Recall, Precision and F-Measure etc for advanced evaluation. These measures are fit for summarized data available in data warehouse environment as described by Zbidi, Faiz, and Limam (2006). Some authors have used conventional measures in past while mining over data warehouses (Kamber et al., 1997; Psaila & Lanzi, 2000; Wei, 2014). There are techniques which use advanced measures of evaluation for pattern extraction and prediction (Messaoud et al., 2006; Messaoud et al., 2007; Usman et al., 2013). The evaluation is more meaningful in these cases as the measures adapted are designed specifically to work with the aggregated data.

In order to provide ability for reviewing extracted patterns through graphical interfaces, visualization techniques have been proposed in literature. However, only few techniques have been developed for visualization part of the process due to the technical aspects of development of such components. These techniques have provided the ability to visualize extracted patterns with the help of column bar graphs, ball graphs and based upon Semiology principals (Zhu, 1998; Bogdanova & Georgieva, 2005: Messaoud et al., 2007).

1.2 UNRESOLVED ISSUES AND MOTIVATION OF THE BOOK

It is apparent that hybrid techniques of extraction and prediction of patterns from large datasets have been under development, but some issues need attention.

Firstly, there are techniques which handle the issue of domain independency by only taking necessary dimensions for the mining process. This way, user is not involved in picking up the dimensions. Some of these techniques are able to reduce the dimensions, however, these results in removing some dimensions having interesting patterns. For instance, one of the techniques doesn't involve user in the feature selection process, but it ranks numeric and nominal data separately. The inter-relation between different types of data is not considered while ranking is done. There is a need to adapt a procedure which can rank both types of data at the same time. By ranking variables at the same time, the relationship within the data is not lost. This way, top ranked variables from whole data set are picked strengthening the ranking process.

Secondly, in past pattern extraction and prediction over data warehouses has not been done at multiple levels in most cases. Usman et al. (2013) has adapted a multi-level approach to mine STAR schema which shows that it is worth mining at multiple levels for business analysts. The schema is generated at cluster level within levels of hierarchy. This process remains cumbersome while mining a large data set, since it has to work at each cluster level to create a schema for mining. Therefore, if a technique is developed to automate this schema generation process, it will strengthen the model. Moreover, it takes a lot of time to manually copy the data from data source to the data warehouse manually, so there is a requirement to create an automated process for moving the data from original source to the data warehouse.

Thirdly, the evaluation of extracted and predicted patterns in these techniques is majorly achieved using conventional measures like Count, Support and Confidence, and Accuracy. These measures were designed to work with the transactional databases only. Researchers have proposed some advanced measures in particular for mining in a data warehouse environment. These measures are based on aggregate data, and thus are more meaningful that the conventional measures. Therefore, there is a strong requirement to evaluate the these models using advanced measures like Rae, Con, Hill, Lift, Loevinger, Precision and F-Measures etc. Moreover, if this process is done at multiple levels of abstraction like in the case of Usman et al. (2013), it becomes cumbersome. The calculation of these measures at every cluster level within each level will not be easy. Therefore, it is recommended that automating this process of calculation of advance measures at multiple levels is done.

Finally, for visualization, it is perceptible that most techniques do not provide visualization whereas it is a helpful addition to the mining process. Some of the techniques however provide this support but at the same time, these are sensitive to large number of rules. Most of these techniques are although able to display the rules in small available space in the interface, but these are not interpretable. Authors have used Ball and Bar Graphs mostly, and it is not easy to distinguish between width and height of balls and bars respectively where researcher has a large resultant set of rules. The approaches which use shades of colors to distinguish rules are also troublesome. It is not easy to differentiate between same shades, as more shades will be used when more rules are generated. Another issue in these techniques is the inability to provide support for showing rules satisfying advanced measures, as most of these only focus support and confidence filters. Therefore, there is a need of visualization component that not only provides ability to show large number of rules in a small space, but also allows researchers to dig out rules using advance measure filters like importance, Rae, Con and Hill etc. For pattern prediction, not many techniques exist for visualization of results, so there is a requirement of visualization component for pattern predictions as well.

The above mentioned issues have motivated to formulate a multi-level pattern extraction and prediction model which is capable to work without domain knowledge requirement, has the ability to work at multiple levels of abstraction, able to evaluate the results using advanced measures and has visualization abilities.

1.3 RESEARCH CHALLENGES CONSIDERED TO BE OUT OF SCOPE

In this section, some of the important research challenges relevant to the work are highlighted which are not addressed due to limited timeframe of the research.

- Firstly, in pattern prediction, ranking is done using normality measure. The process orders the variables in a way that a variable satisfying the normal curve better than the other is given priority. The ranking process is done by creation of normal curves of variables and top ranked variables are picked for further mining process. Any statistical approach is not adapted due limited timescale which involves some statistical evidence for better normality value.

- Secondly, pattern extraction and prediction involves generation of a multi-dimensional schema on third stage. However, only STAR schema has been adapted in these cases. Other schemas like Snowflake and Fact Constellation are not targeted due to short time in MS book.

- Thirdly, the evaluation of classification models is supported by a visualization component. This visualization component allows the analyst to evaluate models one by one. However, for better selection and ease of the user, an interface displaying evaluation measures graphically in a single interface is highly desired. Due to lack of time, an interface with ability to show all models at once was not created.

1.4 PROBLEMS TO BE ADDRESSED

In this book following main research problems are focused:

- To allow pattern extraction and pattern prediction for a given dataset at once. There are techniques for extraction and prediction separately, but no technique exists having both extraction and prediction abilities. It is a challenging research problem.

- To provide an automated process to pick variables for the mining process. This is a significant research problem where data is available in high volume and high number of dimensions. In such cases analysts without domain knowledge also face difficulties in selecting variables.

- To provide pattern extraction and prediction at multiple levels of abstraction rather than on a whole dataset. For high volume data and high number of dimensions, mining at multiple levels involve creation of multi-dimensional schema. The process of schema generation is cumbersome as it is done at each level of abstraction.

- To allow analysts to evaluate the extracted and predicted patterns using advanced measures of interestingness.

- To provide visualization support for the extracted and predicted patterns using a visualization component. Displaying large number of patterns (association rules) in a graphical interface as well as visualization of classification algorithms is a challenging job.

1.5 AIMS AND CONTRIBUTIONS

The title of this book describes the overall objectives of this research work, which is to allow pattern extraction and prediction for environments where data is in large volume and has large number of dimensions. Although some techniques of pattern extraction and prediction in large datasets exist, however these don't allow extraction and prediction abilities at one place. Moreover, both types of techniques have certain issues to be addressed. The basic ideas which determine the contributions of this research work as given below:

- To provide pattern extraction and prediction in a single framework.
- To provide a robust ranking procedure to pick top-ranked variables for mining process in order to minimize the domain knowledge requirement.
- To extract and predict patterns at multiple levels of abstraction with automated support to generate multi-dimensional schema involved in mining process.
- To evaluate the patterns using advanced measures in multi-dimensional environment instead of conventional measures.
- To provide visualization ability to the analysts for better understanding of the extracted patterns.

The main target of this research work is to provide a pattern extraction and prediction framework for analysts by identifying the limitations of the existing approaches and searching for possible options to overcome these limitations. Following main contributions are made in this research work.

- Proposed a methodology that enables the analysts to perform pattern extraction and prediction in same framework with the help of statistical methods, data mining techniques and machine learning algorithms.
- Provided a mechanism to rank variables simultaneously instead of ranking separately for nominal and numeric types.
- Proposed a measure based on normality of data in the variables to rank the most significant variables in a set of variables to select for mining process.
- Provided an algorithm to construct multi-dimensional schema for a given cluster having nominal and numeric variables.
- Provided an algorithm to shift data from the data source to constructed multi-dimensional environment automatically.

- Provided an algorithm to apply advanced measures of interestingness on a set of association rules resulted from pattern extraction process.
- Proposed advanced evaluation of classification algorithms using measures like F-Measure, Precision, Recall etc in multi-dimensional environment.
- Proposed and developed a visualization component for pattern extraction and prediction for better understanding of generated results.
- Performed case studies on three data sets for validation of methodology and showed the effectiveness of the approach. The abilities of domain knowledge independence, multi-level mining, advanced evaluation and visualization are shown in the case studies for all datasets.

1.6 NOVELTY AND SIGNIFICANCE

The research objectives make the proposed methodology novel. To date, there is no systematic study has been done for pattern extraction and prediction framework in paste to investigate the following issues:

- To study the possibility to merge pattern extraction and prediction in large datasets, particularly in data warehouses.
- To provide a mechanism for picking top ranked variables which handles both numeric and nominal variables together.
- To provide algorithms for data warehouse schema generation at multiple levels of abstraction.
- To provide algorithms for calculation of advanced measures at multiple levels of abstraction.
- To provide visualization interface for pattern extraction and prediction process in data warehouse environment.

1.7 BOOK OUTLINE

To address the above mentioned aims and objects of this research, this book is outlined as below:

Chapter 2 provides the literature review of related work done in the context of this research. Section 2.2 provides a review of hybrid approaches of knowledge discovery in large data sets. The section 2.2.1 contains the review of pattern extraction techniques in data warehouse environment. The section 2.2.1.1 provides a review of techniques in context of domain knowledge independence. The section 2.2.1.2 reviews the techniques in terms of their ability to work at multiple levels of abstraction. A detailed review of techniques in terms of domain ability to evaluate using advanced measures is given in section 2.2.1.3. The last section for pattern extraction 2.2.1.4 provides a review of techniques which provided support of visualization for extracted patterns. The section 2.2.2 contains the review of pattern prediction techniques in data warehouse environment. The section 2.2.2.1 provides review of these techniques in terms of domain knowledge independence. The section 2.2.2.2 provides a brief review of techniques working at multiple levels of abstraction. The section 2.2.2.3 reviews the techniques in terms of evaluation methods used. The section 2.3 discusses emerging research and opportunities, and section 2.4 identifies issues in current research. Section 2.5 describes the research objectives and plan for multi-level pattern extraction and prediction. The chapter is concluded in section 2.6.

Chapter 3 is dedicated to explain the proposed model with the help of an example data set. The chapter starts with section 3.1 which explains the framework and provides introduction to the dataset used. The section 3.2 provides an implementation of pattern extraction component having sub-sections involving hierarchical cluster generation, ranking of variables, multidimensional scaling, STAR schema generation, mining and evaluation of association rules, and visualization component. The section 3.3 provides a brief review of pattern prediction. This section has different sub sections for predicting nominal variables, numeric variables and aggregate data separately. The entire sub sections involve detail implementation of prediction steps like clusters generation, ranking of variables, STAR schema generation, implementation and evaluation of classification models as well as visualization and selection of classification models. A summary of this section is presented in section 3.4.

Chapter 4 presents the implementation of the proposed methodology on the first case study done on real-world data set, called Automobile taken from UCI machine learning website. This dataset describes specifications of an automobile with the help of different characteristics, risk ratings and losses information. This data set has a small number of records (205), however it contains 27 variables out of which 11 are nominal and 16 are numeric. Due to mix types of data, this dataset suite the objectives of this research. A detailed implementation of this dataset is done in Chapter 4.

Chapter 5 presents the implementation of the section case study done on a larger data set called Adult having 48, 842 records. The dataset is taken from US Census Bureai website and was submitted to UCI website. It has 8 nominal and 5 numeric variables. A detailed implementation of this dataset is given in chapter 5 based on same lines as in the proposed methodology chapter.

Finally, in chapter 6, the research work is summarized. The contributions of book are described, conclusions are drawn and future research directions are defined in the context of this research work.

REFERENCES

Azeem, M., Usman, M., & Ahmad, W. (2014). *Intelligent data cube construction and exploration.* Paper presented at the Digital Information Management (ICDIM), 2014 Ninth International Conference on. doi:10.1109/ICDIM.2014.6991408

Berson, A., & Smith, S. J. (1997). *Data warehousing, data mining, and OLAP.* McGraw-Hill, Inc.

Bodin-Niemczuk, A., Messaoud, R. B., Rabaséda, S. L., & Boussaid, O. (2008). Vers l'intégration de la prédiction dans les cubes OLAP. *Et gestion des connaissances: EGC'2008.*

Bogdanova, G., & Georgieva, T. (2005). *Discovering the association rules in OLAP data cube with daily downloads of folklore materials.* Paper presented at the International Conference on Computer Systems and Technologies.

Chaudhuri, S., & Dayal, U. (1997). An overview of data warehousing and OLAP technology. *SIGMOD Record, 26*(1), 65–74. doi:10.1145/248603.248616

Chen, Y., Dong, G., Han, J., Pei, J., Wah, B. W., & Wang, J. (2006). Regression cubes with lossless compression and aggregation. *IEEE Transactions on Knowledge and Data Engineering, 18*(12), 1585–1599. doi:10.1109/TKDE.2006.196

Cios, K. J., Pedrycz, W., & Swiniarski, R. W. (1998). *Data Mining and Knowledge Discovery. In Data Mining Methods for Knowledge Discovery* (pp. 1–26). Springer. doi:10.1007/978-1-4615-5589-6

Fayyad, U., Piatetsky-Shapiro, G., & Smyth, P. (1996). From data mining to knowledge discovery in databases. *AI Magazine*, *17*(3), 37.

Frawley, W. J., Piatetsky-Shapiro, G., & Matheus, C. J. (1992). Knowledge discovery in databases: An overview. *AI Magazine*, *13*(3), 57.

Goebel, M., & Gruenwald, L. (1999). A survey of data mining and knowledge discovery software tools. *ACM SIGKDD Explorations Newsletter, 1*(1), 20-33.

Han, J., Kamber, M., & Chiang, J. (1997). *Mining Multi-Dimensional Association Rules Using Data Cubes: Technical report*. Database Systems Research Laboratory, School of Science, Simon Fraser University.

Han, J., Pei, J., & Kamber, M. (2011). *Data mining: concepts and techniques*. Elsevier.

Hand, D. J., Mannila, H., & Smyth, P. (2001). *Principles of data mining*. MIT press.

Hsu, S.-C., & Chien, C.-F. (2007). Hybrid data mining approach for pattern extraction from wafer bin map to improve yield in semiconductor manufacturing. *International Journal of Production Economics*, *107*(1), 88–103. doi:10.1016/j.ijpe.2006.05.015

Kamber, M., Han, J., & Chiang, J. (1997). *Metarule-Guided Mining of Multi-Dimensional Association Rules Using Data Cubes*. Paper presented at the KDD.

Kantardzic, M. (2011). *Data mining: Concepts, models, methods, and algorithms*. John Wiley & Sons. doi:10.1002/9781118029145

Kimball, R., & Caserta, J. (2011). *The Data Warehouse ETL Toolkit: Practical Techniques for Extracting, Cleaning, Conforming, and Delivering Data*. John Wiley & Sons.

Korikache, N., & Yahia, A. (2014). *Coupling OLAP and Data Mining for Prediction*. Academic Press.

Liu, Z., & Guo, M. (2001). *A proposal of integrating data mining and on-line analytical processing in data warehouse*. Paper presented at the Info-tech and Info-net, 2001. doi:10.1109/ICII.2001.983049

McNamara, D. S., Crossley, S. A., Roscoe, R. D., Allen, L. K., & Dai, J. (2015). A hierarchical classification approach to automated essay scoring. *Assessing Writing, 23,* 35–59. doi:10.1016/j.asw.2014.09.002

Messaoud, R. B., Rabaséda, S. L., Boussaid, O., & Missaoui, R. (2006). Enhanced mining of association rules from data cubes. *Proceedings of the 9th ACM international workshop on Data warehousing and OLAP.* doi:10.1145/1183512.1183517

Messaoud, R. B., Rabaséda, S. L., Rokia, M., & Boussaid, O. (2007). OLEMAR: an online environment for mining association rules in multidimensional data. *Data Mining and Knowledge Discovery Technologies, 35.*

Ordonez, C., & Chen, Z. (2009). Evaluating statistical tests on OLAP cubes to compare degree of disease. *IEEE Transactions on Information Technology in Biomedicine, 13*(5), 756–765. doi:10.1109/TITB.2008.926989 PMID:19273013

Palpanas, T. (2000). Knowledge discovery in data warehouses. *SIGMOD Record, 29*(3), 88–100. doi:10.1145/362084.362142

Psaila, G., & Lanzi, P. L. (2000). Hierarchy-based mining of association rules in data warehouses. *Proceedings of the 2000 ACM symposium on Applied computing, 1.* doi:10.1145/335603.335773

Sarawagi, S., Agrawal, R., & Megiddo, N. (1998). *Discovery-driven exploration of OLAP data cubes.* Paper presented at the International Conference on Extending Database Technology.

Usman, M., Asghar, S., & Fong, S. (2009). *A conceptual model for combining enhanced olap and data mining systems.* Paper presented at the INC, IMS and IDC, 2009. NCM'09. Fifth International Joint Conference on. doi:10.1109/NCM.2009.354

Usman, M., Pears, R., & Fong, A. C. M. (2013). Discovering diverse association rules from multidimensional schema. *Expert Systems with Applications, 40*(15), 5975–5996. doi:10.1016/j.eswa.2013.05.031

Wang, X. Z. (1999). *Data Mining and Knowledge Discovery—an Overview. In Data Mining and Knowledge Discovery for Process Monitoring and Control* (pp. 13–28). Springer. doi:10.1007/978-1-4471-0421-6_2

Wei, H. (2014). *Study on a data warehouse mining oriented fuzzy association rule mining algorithm.* Paper presented at the Intelligent Systems Design and Engineering Applications (ISDEA), 2014 Fifth International Conference on. doi:10.1109/ISDEA.2014.207

Yadav, D., & Pal, S. (2015). An Integration of Clustering and Classification Technique in Software Error Detection. *African Journal of Computing and ICT, 8*(2).

You, J., Dillon, T., & Liu, J. (2001). *An integration of data mining and data warehousing for hierarchical multimedia information retrieval.* Paper presented at the Intelligent Multimedia, Video and Speech Processing. doi:10.1109/ISIMP.2001.925411

Zbidi, N., Faiz, S., & Limam, M. (2006). On mining summaries by objective measures of interestingness. *Machine Learning, 62*(3), 175–198. doi:10.1007/s10994-005-5066-8

Zhu, H. (1998). *On-line analytical mining of association rules.* Simon Fraser University.

Chapter 2
Literature Review

ABSTRACT

The purpose of this literature review chapter is to discuss the integrated techniques of knowledge discovery, identify gaps, and draw research objectives of this research. The chapter firstly discusses the pattern extraction techniques from large datasets, for example, a data warehouse, followed by pattern prediction techniques. A review of pattern extraction and prediction is presented on the basis of knowledge independency, multi-level mining ability, advanced evaluation of results, and visualization ability. At the end, a summary of issues in the current research are presented followed by the research objectives of this research.

2.1 INTRODUCTION

Chapter 2 provides the literature review of related work done in the context of this research. Section 2.2 provides a review of hybrid approaches of knowledge discovery in large data sets. The section 2.2.1 contains the review of pattern extraction techniques in data warehouse environment. The section 2.2.1.1 provides a review of techniques in context of domain knowledge independence. The section 2.2.1.2 reviews the techniques in terms of their ability to work at multiple levels of abstraction. A detailed review of techniques in terms of domain ability to evaluate using advanced measures is given in section 2.2.1.3. The last section for pattern extraction 2.2.1.4 provides a review of techniques which provided support of visualization for extracted patterns. The section 2.2.2 contains the review of pattern prediction techniques in data warehouse environment. The section 2.2.2.1 provides review of these techniques in terms of domain knowledge independence. The section 2.2.2.2

DOI: 10.4018/978-1-5225-5029-7.ch002

provides a brief review of techniques working at multiple levels of abstraction. The section 2.2.2.3 reviews the techniques in terms of evaluation methods used. The section 2.3 discusses emerging research and opportunities, and section 2.4 identifies issues in current research. Section 2.5 describes the research objectives and plan for multi-level pattern extraction and prediction. The chapter is concluded in section 2.6.

2.2 HYBRID TECHNIQUES OF KNOWLEDGE DISCOVERY

Knowledge discovery from large datasets has remained an interesting domain for researchers. Analysts have been interested in finding hidden and interesting patterns from large data sets (Frawley, Piatetsky-Shapiro, & Matheus, 1992;Fayyad, Piatetsky-Shapiro, & Smyth, 1996;Goebel & Gruenwald, 1999). For knowledge discovery data mining and data warehousing have played a major role independently (Cios, Pedrycz, & Swiniarski, 1998;Wang, 1999; Palpanas, 2000). Data mining has widely been used for knowledge discovery in all domains like business, medicine,, education and science as it aims to extract patterns from large data sets (Han, Kamber, & Chiang, 1997;Hand, Mannila, & Smyth, 2001). On the other hand data warehouses have been used for exploratory analysis by the researchers. Researchers have worked in past for data warehouse evolution in various directions (Kimball & Caserta, 2011;Berson & Smith, 1997; Chaudhuri & Dayal, 1997). However recently, researchers have started using both domains in hybrid fashion (You, Dillon, & Liu, 2001;Z. Liu & Guo, 2001; Chen et al., 2006; Hsu & Chien, 2007; Messaoud, Rabaséda, Boussaid, & Missaoui, 2006;Messaoud, Rabaséda, Rokia, & Boussaid, 2007;;,Korikache & Yahia, 2014). The hybrid techniques are generally used for knowledge discovery and have strengthened the process.

Han, Pei, and Kamber (2011) have defined different characteristics of a mining processing working in a multidimensional environment. Authors have suggested that mining process needs to be domain independent, so that analysts can use the process without domain knowledge. Secondly, a good mining process provides facilities for mining on different subsets of data and at varying levels of abstraction in a multi-dimensional environment. The extracted knowledge needs to be validated through advanced measures of interestingness as well. Moreover, the process is strengthened by adding a visualization component to the process.

It is interesting that hybrid techniques of knowledge discovery have been used for knowledge discovery in almost all domains in past. For example Bogdanova and Georgieva (2005) used hybrid approach for pattern extraction from archived funds with folklore materials of a folklore institute. Recently, Yadav and Pal (2015) also used a hybrid mining approach in software error detection. The approach included classification techniques in a data warehouse environment. Similarly, McNamara, Crossley, Roscoe, Allen, and Dai (2015) used hybrid approach to propose a technique for automated scoring. Few authors have also worked out for hybrid techniques in medical domain (Messaoud et al.,2006; Messaoud et al., 2007; Ordonez & Chen, 2009; Bodin-Niemczuk, Messaoud, Rabaséda, & Boussaid, 2008). In some cases, it is important for a knowledge discovery to be guided by a domain expert. In this area, approaches have been proposed in which user guides the mining process while working in a data warehouse environment (Kamber, Han, & Chiang, 1997; Messaoud et al., 2006; Messaoud et al., 2007; Ordonez &Chen, 2009; Kamber et al., 1997; Sarawagi, Agrawal, & Megiddo, 1998). There are some approaches which mine over data warehouse in automated way (Usman, Pears, & Fong, 2013; Ordonez & Chen, 2009; Azeem, Usman, & Ahmad, 2014). The inclusion of such automated support makes it possible to find hidden patterns existing in the data.

As described by Han et al. (2011), another important feature of a mining process is the ability to work at multiple levels of abstraction. This ability allows a researcher to explore the data at different levels. While mining in a multi-dimensional environment, not many techniques exist which work at multiple levels of abstraction. Few techniques allow pattern extraction from data warehouses with the help of hierarchical clustering (Azeem et al., 2014; Korikache & Yahia, 2014). Similarly, pattern prediction has also been done at multiple levels with the help of hierarchical clustering. These approaches work at multiple levels of abstraction and have the ability to extract and predict patterns (Zhu, 1998; Wang et al., 2013; Usman et al., 2013). These techniques have shown the potential of hybrid approaches in knowledge discovery at multiple levels.

Similarly, Han and Kamber think that a mining process must evaluate the knowledge at the end of the process. Patterns extracted and predicted from a data mining process are normally evaluated at the last stage in a multidimensional mining environment. Since data mining methods were initially supported for mining over transaction databases, therefore the techniques for evaluation were majorly based on conventional measures like support, confidence, and accuracy. However, while mining in a multidimensional environment, data is available in aggregate form, so authors have proposed measures like Lift, Loevinger, Rae, Con, Hill, Recall, Precision and F-Measure etc for advanced evaluation. These measures are fit for summarized data available in data warehouse environment as described by Zbidi, Faiz, and Limam (2006). Some authors have used conventional measures in past while mining over data warehouses (Kamber et al., 1997; Psaila & Lanzi, 2000; Wei, 2014). There are techniques which use advanced measures of evaluation for pattern extraction and prediction (Messaoud et al., 2006; Messaoud et al., 2007; Usman et al., 2013). The evaluation is more meaningful in these cases as the measures adapted are designed specifically to work with the aggregated data.

In order to facilitate the researchers for reviewing extracted patterns through graphical interfaces, visualization techniques have been proposed in literature. Researchers in past have provided interfaces where it is possible to interpret and analyze extracted patterns graphically. In case of hybrid techniques, few researchers have worked for visualization part of the process due to the technical aspects of development of such interfaces. These techniques have provided the ability to visualize extracted patterns with the help of column bar graphs, ball graphs and based upon Semiology principals (Zhu, 1998; Bogdanova & Georgieva, 2005; Messaoud et al., 2007). However, there is no technique which can deal with the large number of patterns extracted from the mining process effectively.

2.2.1 Pattern Extraction From Large Datasets

As described above, pattern extraction is one of the major areas of knowledge discovery from large data sets. Extraction of patterns form large datasets remains a challenge for analysts (Fayyad et al., 1996; Xingdon Wu, Zhu, Wu, & Ding, 2014) due to the large number of dimensions and volume. Researchers have proposed algorithms and techniques in past for pattern extraction over large datasets (Goebel &Gruenwald, 1999; Dong & Li, 1999). Association rule mining is one of the techniques in which patterns from data sets are extracted in the form of rules (Agrawal, Imielinski, and Swami, 1993). Many algorithms exist in literature, which enable researchers to mine association rules form data sets. Some of the well-known algorithms are *Apriori, Partition-Algorithm, FP-Growth* and *Eclat* as cited by Hipp, Güntzer, and Nakhaeizadeh (2000). These algorithms were originally designed and tested on transactional databases, and were optimized in great deal. Data warehouses have made it possible to store large volume of data for analysis purposes. Recently, large data sets are available in data warehouse environment and can be used for mining purposes. Association rule mining techniques have been applied by researchers in past over data warehouses (Kamber et al., 1997; Messaoud et al., 2006; Messaoud et al., 2007; Usman et al., 2013). According to Kamber et al. (1997), it is interesting to mine multi-dimensional association rules to find relationships among multiple dimensions in data warehouses.

In past, association rule mining over data warehouses has been done in two ways. Researchers have applied association rule mining on the data warehouse schema called STAR schema (Zhu, 1998; Psaila & Lanzi, 2000; Usman et al., 2013) to extract hidden and interesting patterns. The other method is to apply association rule mining over data cubes available in the data warehouses (Kamber et al., 1997; Bogdanova & Georgieva, 2005; Messaoud et al., 2006; Ordonez & Chen, 2009; Wei, 2014).

Although data warehouses are mainly built using either Snowflake schema and STAR schema, but researchers have majorly targeted STAR schema. Since the STAR schema contains the relationships in the form of a fact table and multiple dimensions, it is best suited for mining purposes (Psaila and Lanzi, 2000). The research in past focused to mine association rules from STAR schema in two ways. Some techniques generated the schema in a way that mining over it yielded better results, i.e by using more important dimensions. The other way was to mine association rules over an existing schema. In past, few techniques like SAMSTAR were proposed to generate STAR schema directly from a relational database diagram called an ERD (Song et al., 2008). The technique was able to minimize the effort of creating a data warehouse schema manually. However it remained impossible to create a schema, so that it only contains most important dimensions for the fact table and thus helps in the mining process afterwards. So authors have recently focused in the automated generation of STAR schema (Usman et al., 2013) for mining purposes. Authors have also proposed to exploit the STAR schema at multiple levels of abstraction in past. Moreover, the well-known association rule mining algorithm called *Apriori* has majorly been used in most of the techniques. It also important to note that, in these techniques the evaluation criteria followed by most of the authors has followed conventional measures of interestingness which were actually developed for transactional databases. Another aspect is the visualization of extracted patterns. No technique, while mining from STAR schema, has provided insights to the extracted patterns by using a graphical component.

Data cubes store the data in the data warehouses in aggregate form. These cubes can be exploited in order to mine association rules (Kamber et al., 1997;

Bogdanova & Georgieva, 2005; Messaoud et al., 2006). In some techniques in past, researchers have emphasized on the role of users to guide the mining process (Kamber et al., 1997; Messaoud et al., 2006) where as in some cases the process itself picked the dimensions for mining (Bogdanova & Georgieva, 2005; Ordonez & Chen, 2009). Authors have also applied this techniques at multiple levels of abstraction in past. Like mining using STAR schema, this type of mining has also majorly been done using *Apriori* Algorithm. Moreover, the evaluation of extracted patterns in some cases has been done using advanced measures like Messaoud et al. (2006). Unlike the techniques using STAR Schema, these techniques have provided ability to visualize the extracted patterns at the end. However some issues of visualization of large number of rules exist in available techniques (Zhu, 1998; Messaoud et al., 2006). It is also important to mention here that the some techniques in this type of mining were developed for specific domains like Folklore data sets (Bogdanova & Georgieva, 2005) and disease diagnosis data set (Ordonez & Chen, 2009). Most of the techniques in this type of mining were generalized using real world data sets from UCI Machine Learning website.

As discussed at the start of this chapter, Han and Kamber dicsused different aspects of a mining process implemented in multidimensional environment. First aspect is the ability to extract and predict patterns without requirement of domain knowledge. The mining process with this ability do not require a domain expert to be involved in the mining process in order to guide it and the extracted patterns are always interesting. The second aspect is to mine at multiple levels of abstraction which allows to mine at different levels of hierarchy, enabling the extraction of patterns at all levels instead of the top level only. Another aspect of mining process in multidimensional environment is that, it ensures that the extracted and predicted patterns are evaluated using advanced measures instead of conventional measures. Finally, the extracted and predicted patterns are represented with the help of a visualization component allowing the analysts to interact and explore the patterns graphically. A review of pattern extraction techniques is presented on the basis of these four aspects.

2.2.1.1 Domain Knowledge Independency

In past, techniques have emerged in which user was able to guide the mining process to find patterns. In these cases, the process is assisted by users so that mining process only looks for specific regions in the data set rather than the whole data set. This allows mining of interesting patterns. However, when it comes to mining hidden patterns which are interesting for the researchers, the mining process should have the ability to find patterns without human intervention. In these cases, the process should be automated in some way to look for interesting patterns itself. A review of techniques for pattern extraction in the form of association rules is presented keeping in view the requirement of domain knowledge independency.

Meta rule guided mining on data cubes was used by Kamber et al. (1997) in order to create a smaller subset of data as input for rule mining process. Meta rules are provided by the business analysts before the mining process is started. The mining process is guided by such rules for a meaningful cube construction in the next phase. This approach is interactive in nature for the user, where user can provide the hypothesis in the shape of a meta-rule or pattern template. During mining process, only those patterns are considered which confirm the hypothesis drawn by the user. That way, it increases the chances of finding interesting patterns for the user as well as constrains the search space for the mining process to make it more efficient. Two algorithms are provided by the authors to serve this purpose. First algorithm, called n-D Cube search, works when data cube is available for searching purposes. Second algorithm works in case the data cube is not available, and it creates the cube first. Authors term the second algorithm as multi-p-D Cube Construction Algorithm. Although the technique always provides meaningful results to the business analysts, however technical knowledge is required to create meta rules. Moreover, such methodology may not suite in the cases, where business analysts are interested in finding hidden patterns.

In a similar approach Bogdanova and Georgieva (2005) worked on provision of selection of interesting dimensions with a minimum support value. The authors presented a method to discover association rules from specific data cubes called *FolkloreCubes* which are created from an archival fund with folklore materials of Folklore Institute. The data cube *FolkloreCube* is created by using a WEB based client/server system that contains an archival fund with folklore materials of the Folklore Institute. This particular cube contains four dimensions namely Document, Link, User and Time. The authors created an application to generate these cubes and provided an interface to the user to select the interesting dimensions with a minimum support value. The procedure generates frequent item sets which are further used in the rule generation process. User can provide minimum confidence for this step. Authors have also provided a way to visualize the generated rules. Although authors were able to strengthen the mining process, but the methodology depends upon conventional support measure as well as it was only tested on specific types of cubes i.e *FolkloreCubes* and has not been generalized. Similar to the previous approach, this technique is also user-driven, and doesn't discover hidden patterns.

Moving forward with the approach adapted by Kamber et al. (1997), Messaoud et al. (2006) used meta-rules approach for extracting association rules from data cubes in a multi-dimensional environment. Their mining process is guided by a meta-rule context driven by analysis objectives and thus helps to draw rules which are meaningful for the analysts. These meta-rules are called inter-dimensional meta-rules by the authors as inter-dimensional associations can be extended to large application domains like data warehouses. The generated rules are evaluated using advanced measures like *Lift* and *Loevinger*. Authors aim to extend their model to work with intra-dimensional rules. Although the generated rules are interesting for the users, due to context-driven approach, but the approach is not suitable for the domains where hidden patterns are to be extracted. Moreover, development of meta-rules and pattern templates becomes technical aspect of the mining process, and thus technical abilities are required for this approach. Normally, domain experts are not very technical to create such meta rules without technical assistance.

Next year, authors Messaoud et al. (2007) used same approach in their enhanced research for meta-rule guided mining. The new system was called as OLEMAR (On-Line Environment for Mining Association Rules) which is an enhancement of previous work focusing meta-rule guided mining of association rules. In the enhanced version, a complete online mining environment was created which included previous work as well as ability to visualize the generated patterns. In the enhanced version, authors used same context-driven meta rules and pattern templates to guide the mining process. Like the approach presented by Kamber et al. (1997), and author's previous limited version (Messaoud et al. (2006)), this complete system is also guided by the user, and thus doesn't look for hidden interesting patterns. Moreover, similar to the previous approaches, it also requires technical knowledge to deal with the meta-rule and pattern templates required in the process.

Rather than using the meta-rule guided approaches, Ordonez and Chen (2009) applied statistical methods on data cubes in order to improve disease diagnostics. In order to find out the significant differences in facts by identifying the dimensions which are dissimilar to the others, authors proposed data cube exploration using parametric statistical techniques. Domain knowledge requirement becomes important in such cases for pointing out the regions where such significant fact differences are suspected. Therefore, this approach is not suited in cases, where domain experts are looking for hidden patterns. Another issue with the technique in discussion is the difficulty in working with optimization methods, which are hard for domain experts, so these cannot be adapted without technical assistance. Moreover, authors worked only for improvement in disease diagnostics and their target was not to achieve a general technique for mining association rules which could be utilized in all domains. So it is not evident as if these techniques will perform in similar fashion for all datasets.

In a different approach, Psaila and Lanzi (2000) designed a technique for analysts to guide the mining process towards interesting mining queries by exploiting the concept hierarchies available in the multidimensional structure. This methodology not only works with the explicit concept hierarchies driven from the multidimensional schema, but also works with implicit concept hierarchies which are inducted by semantic generalization of relationships within attributes. The complexity of the data in this case is decreased, as mining process is guided towards interesting mining queries, disregarding the useless queries. The approach is meta-rule dependent, as these are required at the start of the process for each level in the hierarchy. The approach is also limited in nature due to the emphasis on technical knowledge of the user as well as the requirement of domain knowledge. These limitations do not allow exploring hidden interesting patterns using this approach.

Due to the issues pointed out in the previous approaches above, Usman et al. (2013) worked out on a technique which didn't require domain knowledge to explore patterns. The aim of the approach was to extract patterns at multiple levels without domain knowledge. To serve this purpose, authors created data warehouse schema at each level and mined association rules from it. The schema was based on only important dimensions in the data, which were picked, be statistical methods. Authors used Principal Component Analysis (PCA) for ranking numeric variables in the data, where as Information Gain was used to rank nominal variables. The rules generated using this approach was found to be more interesting than *Apriori* Algorithm applied on the actual data in terms of diversity measure. This approach doesn't require the experts to have domain knowledge as well as technical expertise is not involved to extract the patterns. However, since two different approaches are used to pick dimensions for multi-dimensional schema, the relationship in the data is not considered and the process becomes ambiguous. The technique ranks numeric variables separately using PCA whereas nominal data is ranked separately using Information. Both ranking procedures do not consider the other type of data while ranking, thus the relationship between both types of data is not considered during ranking. Therefore the ranking process becomes ambiguous.

It is evident that most of the above approaches required researcher to guide the mining process (Kamber et al. (1997), Messaoud et al. (2006), Messaoud et al. (2007), Ordonez and Chen (2009)). Since in these cases user guides the mining process, it results in only known patterns and now hidden knowledge is discovered. Firstly, user must be a domain expert, so that he/she can guide the process towards the required patterns. Secondly, user must have enough technical knowledge to develop required meta-rules and pattern templates or should be assisted in some way to develop these. Moreover, these techniques only find interesting patterns, so these are not suited for the domains where hidden knowledge is important. Apart from this particular issue, some techniques are only tested and validated using typical data sets like the approaches of (Bogdanova and Georgieva (2005)) and (Ordonez and Chen (2009)). The target of these techniques was to find a solution for a particular data set and therefore authors didn't focus on generalizing these approaches. Moreover, its not clear as if these approaches will be suited for data with mixed types of attributes, high number of dimensions and large volume. One of the approaches, recently was able to find hidden interesting patterns without human intervention (Usman et al. (2013)), but it also has a limitation in the ranking process. It doesn't consider the underlying relationship between didn't types of data while ranking, and thus becomes ambiguous. The summary of these approaches is provided in the Table 1. There is a strong requirement of a model that is able to resolve the issues pointed above in a multidimensional environment.

2.2.1.2 Multi-Level Association Rule Mining

Application of association rule mining on the whole dataset or data warehouse at top level provides the ability to find hidden patterns at top level. However there are cases where researchers are interested to find hidden patterns at multiple levels of abstraction. A number of techniques are available in literature which enabled analysts to generate association rules at multiple levels of abstraction in transactional databases. However, not many authors in the past have worked for association rule mining at multiple levels in data warehouses.

Zhu (1998) proposed an approach to perform multi-level association rule mining on different levels of dimensional hierarchy. Such approach mines three

Table 1. Summary of techniques for domain knowledge independency

Authors	Title	Technique Used	Model	Limitations
Kamber et al. (1997)	Association rule mining on data cubes	Users can guide the mining process with the help of meta rules and pattern-templates.	Data Cubes	Requires technical ability to create meta-rules. Generates only known patterns.
Bogdanova and Georgieva (2005)	Discovering the association rules in OLAP data cube with daily downloads of folklore materials	Selection of interesting dimensions with a minimum support value	Data Cubes	User driven approach which is unable to find hidden patterns and validates results using support measures which is suited for transactional databases only.
Messaoud et al. (2006)	Enhanced mining of association rules from data cubes	User can guide the mining process with the help of meta-rules and pattern templates.	Data Cubes	Requires technical knowledge to guide the mining process, and results are also known patterns only.
Messaoud et al. (2007)	OLEMAR: An On-Line Environment for Mining Association Rules in Multidimensional Data	User can guide the mining process with the help of meta-rules and pattern templates.	Data Cubes	The approach is only tested on medical datasets, and also drives only user-driven patterns.
Ordonez and Chen (2009)	Evaluating statistical tests on OLAP cubes to compare degree of disease.	Statistical methods to find significant dimensions	Data Cubes	Requires technical knowledge to run statistical tests to find significant dimensions.
Psaila and Lanzi (2000)	Hierarchy-based mining of association rules in data warehouses	User can guide the mining process with the help of meta-rules and pattern templates.	STAR Schema	Based on meta rules which become user-driven and doesn't generate hidden patterns.
Usman et al. (2013)	Discovering diverse association rules from multidimensional schema	Automatically picking the important dimensions for cube construction	STAR Schema	Ranks nominal and numeric variables separately causing ambiguity in the ranking process

types of multidimensional rules namely intra-dimensional, inter-dimensional and hybrid association rules. Intra-dimensional association is association in a single dimension, and in this case, rules from a single dimension are considered. Inter-dimensional rules are extracted using multiple dimensions where as hybrid association rules combine the first two types of rules. The authors have developed algorithms for mining these types of rules in their data mining tool called DBMiner. In all cases, the process drills down or rolls up for selected dimension along with the concept hierarchy to the required level, and then finds association rules at the new level of abstraction using mining algorithms.

Continuing with multi-level mining using concept hierarchies, Wang (1999) presented a multi-level algorithm which worked with data cubes. The author aimed at improving computational time of *Apriori* Algorithm for mining association rules using data cubes. They enlist deficiencies in existing association rule mining algorithms in transactional databases. Such deficiencies include large candidate item set generation, redundant association rules and inability to work with dimension hierarchies. The proposed algorithm makes use of concept hierarchies to dynamically adjust the dimension hierarchy. Authors also used Hash technology to optimize the mining algorithm. The algorithm also includes a step to deal with redundant rules. The performance of algorithm is compared with *Apriori* Algorithm and computational time is reported to be decreased. The primary focus of this technique is to reduce the computational time, however further evaluation for interestingness is required.

Instead of working with concept hierarchy, Usman et al. (2013) used agglomerative hierarchical clustering to mine at multiple levels of abstraction. The authors created multi-dimensional schema at multiple levels of abstraction at each cluster level. This allowed authors to mine association rules on the schema at multiple levels, rather than the whole data set. The approach was tested using synthetic data sets, and it was compared with the results obtained by apply mining on the actual data. The approach was able to generate more important rules generated from schema than the data. Due to the large data used in the data sets, authors made use of sampling to achieve clusters at multiple levels in lesser time, and then mapped remaining instances in each cluster by finding *Euclidean* distance. This approach is well suited for the datasets in large number of dimensions and volume. However it only works with numerical data in order to generate clusters. The nominal variables are not involved in cluster generation process.

From the review of above approaches, it appears that analysts find it useful if the mining process is done at multiple levels. The concept provided by Zhu (1998) was followed by some authors, however it was not continued. This approach exploited the explicit and implicit concept hierarchies. In return, it allowed finding patterns at multiple levels of abstraction. As per discussion above, recently Usman et al. (2013) worked at multiple levels of abstraction while mining association rules. Their approach uses Agglomerative Hierarchical Clustering to create clusters at multiple levels of abstraction. This way, it allows to mine at multiple levels. Authors generated STAR schema at each cluster level and found the approach promising. In this case if an instance is incorrectly put in a wrong cluster in early stages in the process, it cannot be moved to the other cluster later. The summary of these approaches is provided in the Table 2. Exploration of approaches for multi-level mining of association rules is further desired.

2.2.1.3 Advanced Evaluation of Extracted Patterns

Evaluation of association rules is an important step in the mining process while mining from transactional databases. Evaluation is done using measures like Count, Support and Confidence etc. These measures enable to evaluate if the extracted patterns are important and interesting in the underlying data. However, these measures are only meant to work with the transactional databases as described by Zbidi et al. (2006). The authors emphasized on the usage of advanced measures of interestingness when evaluating the aggregate data available in a multi-dimensional environment in a mining process. A review of some techniques adapted by researchers has been presented which aim to evaluate association rules driven from data warehouses.

Kamber et al. (1997) designed a methodology utilizing the thresholds called support and confidence in each dimension in the data cube. The methodology comprises of few algorithms. These algorithms use data cube structure in order to extract knowledge in form of association rules. The m-D slicing algorithm as developed by the authors uses thresholds called support and confidence in each dimension in the data cube. To find large item sets. The process filters the rules based on confidence values. The process generates a cube if it's not present already. During the process of cube construction, another algorithm prunes records in order to find large

Table 2. Summary of techniques for multi-level association rule mining

Authors	Title	Multi-Level Approach Used	Model	Limitations
Zhu (1998)	On-line analytical mining of association rules	Intra-dimensional, inter-dimensional and hybrid association rules mining by exploiting concept hierarchies	Data Cubes	Doesn't take advantage of hierarchical levels of dimensions as data cubes are flattened to mine rules.
Wang (1999)	Mining association rules from stars	Exploited the concept hierarchies to achieve multi-level mining	STAR Schema	Becomes expensive in computation in case of large volume data.
Usman et al. (2013)	Discovering diverse association rules from multidimensional schema	Used agglomerative hierarchical clustering to create clusters at multiple levels for mining purposes	STAR Schema	Inability to correct miss-classification or a stage in future stages of the mining process

item sets. This algorithm works on a smaller set at the end of generation of association rules. Authors have shown that the algorithm works better than Apriori Algorithm. Authors used traditional measures in order to evaluate the interestingness and it's not evident as if the generated rules with better confidence and support values were actually meaningful for the business analysts or not. Moreover, such measures were initially proposed for mining on transactional databases and not necessarily applicable on data cubes as data cubes contain aggregated information.

In another approach Wei (2014) also used conventional measures i.e Support and Confidence as part of the evaluation process in the algorithm during the generation of fuzzy association rules from the data in data warehouse. First step builds the basic data source with the help of hierarchy trees and fuzzy set tables. In the second step large scale item sets from this data are generated. The last step involves the association rules generation by using fuzzy rules generating algorithm. The proposed algorithm has been evaluated using Adult dataset from UCI machine learning repository. This approach also emphasize on Support and Confidence measures like the previous approach above. As described earlier as well, these conventional measures were proposed for mining in transactional databases and are not applicable where data is available in summarized form like data cubes. It becomes interesting to see the effectiveness of this algorithm after evaluation using advanced measures described by Zbidi et al. (2006) which are applicable for aggregated data.

Following the guidelines provided Zbidi et al. (2006), two advanced measures were used by Messaoud et al. (2006). The authors presented a methodology which works over data cubes in a multi-dimensional environment. The process works with meta-rule guided approach as described previously. This process is guided by the users with the help of meta rules and pattern templates. Authors targeted inter-dimensional rules and evaluated these using advanced measures called Lift and Loevinger. These measures provide the relevance of rules more accurately than support and confidence as these are meant for aggregated data. This approach was tested with sales data and was reported to be effective. The results encouraged the researchers towards a complete mining environment based on this algorithm by deploying few more components.

This new environment was called as OLEMAR (Online Environment for Mining Association Rules) in the study of Messaoud et al. (2007). In this novel approach, authors created a complete environment for mining inter-dimensional association rules from data cubes using meta-rule guide approach like before. These rules were validated with advanced measures called Lift and *Loevinger* as in the previous approach. Authors provided a visual support to this environment, and presented both Lift and *Loevinger* in the graphical component. High value of *Lift* measure was represented using low luminosity of Blue Square against the rule; whereas high values of *Loevinger* were represented using low luminosity of red triangle against the rule. This approach is tested with clinical data dealing with the breast cancer research domain. The data contained approximately 2 600 studies, where each study corresponded to a patient case.

In a different approach for evaluation of interestingness of extracted patterns, Psaila and Lanzi (2000) designed a custom metric. This technique allows analysts to guide the mining process towards interesting mining queries by exploiting the concept hierarchies available in the multidimensional structure. This methodology not only works with the explicit concept hierarchies driven from the multidimensional schema, but also works with implicit concept hierarchies which are inducted by semantic generalization of relationships within attributes. This process is guided by meta-rules and pattern templates provided by the user. The mined association rules are evaluated using a custom metric which ensures that meta-pattern exploiting the hierarchies can generate useful rule sets. The evaluation metric was created for sales data specifically and was not generalized for all types of data. Therefore, it limits the usage of such metric for any other type of data. Moreover, the metric is not based upon the aggregated data, but was defined specifically for pattern templates. It is not possible to use this metric in other types of mining where meta-rules and pattern templates are not used.

In order to make use of advanced measures of interestingness Usman et al. (2013), worked out with diversity criteria in their multi-level association rule mining approach. This approach generates STAR schema at multiple levels in the hierarchy. This schema is then used for mining association rules. Authors have used importance measure to provide top rules generated from this approach. Moreover, authors have used three of the diversity measures namely Rae, CON and Hill in order to evaluate the interestingness of generated rules. This approach was tested on synthetic data sets taken from UCI Machine Learning Repository. The diversity achieved using this approach was found to be better than the diversity achieved y generating rules from original data. According to authors, as assured by Zbidi et al. (2006), such advanced measures are fit for usage in multi-dimensional environment and thus confirm the interestingness level better than traditional measures. Further exploration of diversity measures will be interesting to examine.

From the review of evaluation measures of interestingness of association rules in multi-dimensional environment, it is clear that the conventional measures like Count, Support and Confidence remain dominant in many cases. In these cases, the results are ambiguous as these measures are not meant to work with the aggregate data (Kamber et al. (1997), Wei (2014). Moreover, in some cases, custom created metrics were used to measure interestingness. The technique used by Psaila and Lanzi (2000) in this kind of methodologies is not applicable due to the fact that it was created specifically for meta rules and pattern templates. Recently, few authors have started using advanced measures of interestingness like Lift, Loevinger, Rae, CON and Hill etc (Messaoud et al. (2006), Messaoud et al. (2007), Usman et al. (2013)). These measures are bested suited for summarized data present in the data warehouse environment. The summary of the above mentioned approaches is presented in the Table 3. Therefore, there is a strong need to use these advanced measures while mining association rules in a multi-dimensional environment.

Table 3. Evaluation techniques in association rule mining in data warehouses

Authors	Title	Evaluation Method	Model	Limitations
Kamber et al. (1997)	Association rule mining on data cubes	Provided interestingness measure for rules using support and confidence measures.	Data Cubes	Support and Confidence measures of interestingness are used.
Wei (2014)	Study on a data warehouse mining oriented fuzzy association rule mining algorithm	Provided interestingness measure for rules using support and confidence measures.	Data Cubes	Only Fuzzy based association rule mining has been done.
Messaoud et al. (2006)	Enhanced mining of association rules from data cubes	Used Lift and Loevinger criteria for evaluation of interestingness	Data Cubes	The approach has only been validated on specific dataset.
Messaoud et al. (2007)	OLEMAR: An On-Line Environment for Mining Association Rules in Multidimensional Data	Used Lift and Loevinger criteria for evaluation of interestingness	Data Cubes	Medical dataset has been used for implementation and testing only.
Psaila Psaila and Lanzi (2000)	Hierarchy-based mining of association rules in data warehouses	Created a custom metric for evaluation of association rules generated from data warehouse.	STAR Schema	Custom metric for a particular domain is used, and it's not generalized for all data sets.
Usman et al. (2013)	Discovering diverse association rules from multidimensional schema	Used Rae, CON, Hill (diversity measures) of interestingness.	STAR Schema	Top-ranked variables are selected for Schema using a process where nominal and numeric data is ranked separately.

2.2.1.4 Visualization of Identified Patterns

A data mining process can be strengthened by the usage of a visualization component at the end of the mining process which allows analysts to visualize the generated patterns. Techniques exist in literature to visualize association rules generated from datasets. Some techniques are available for transactional databases. For example, Sekhavat and Hoeber (2013) has provided visualization ability with the help of Linked Matrices, Graphs and Detailed views in a transactional database environment. Castillo-Rojas, Vargas, and Villegas (2014) has recently used Self-Organizing Map (SOM) technique for visualization of association rules. *AssocExplorer* tool which was designed by G. Liu et al. (2012) also provides ability to visualize association rules. There are many other approaches which enable researchers to graphically inspect the results, but these work specifically on databases. Recently few authors have targeted visualization at the end of the mining process from data warehouses (either done using data cubes or star schema). A review of these techniques is presented below:

During the process of mining association rules from data cubes, Zhu (1998) assisted the process with the help of a visualization component. The approach performs multi-level association rule mining on different levels of dimensional hierarchy. Such approach mines three types of multidimensional rules namely intra-dimensional, inter-dimensional and hybrid association rules. The process is assisted with the help of a graphical component with two types of graphs. Ball graph provides the association rule representation with balls and line-arrows, where ball represents the frequent item and line-arrow represents one rule. The width of arrow head defines the confidence of that rule, and the width of arrow represents the support of the particular rule. Bar Graph puts items on both axes, with rule height represents the support of rule, and color represents the confidence of rule. In both visualization techniques, the huge number of rules might not be easy to interpret. In case of ball graph, it is not easy to differentiate between different arrows based upon their widths in a galaxy of rules. Similarly, the arrow heads are not easy to interpret when rules are large in numbers. The space required for bar graph has the same issue; it is not possible to interpret large number of rules in this graph in small space. Moreover, it is not evident as how many colors are used to provide insights to rules based upon their confidence value. Different color shades are not easy to interpret when rules are large in numbers.

Another similar approach based upon bar graphs was presented by Bogdanova and Georgieva (2005) who showed association rules using a column-bar graph. The method is used to discover association rules from specific data cubes called *FolkloreCubes* which are created from an archival fund with folklore materials of Folklore Institute. By the end of mining process, a tabular set of rules is generated along with a visual column-bar graph for the user. Each row in the table contains information of a single rule including support and confidence. The authors have provided an interface to the users to filter/sort these rules based upon support and confidence. Authors suggest that the tabular view is important in case of large number of rules generated from the mining process. However, tabular view may not provide a comprehensive view of relationships between rules and items. In order to overcome this issue, authors provided a graphical interface which intends to show a clear picture of all rules. In graph, each rule is presented by a column where height of the column denotes the support of that rule. However it may become difficult in terms of visualization when it comes to visualize too many rules at once, since there may be different rules having more or less similar support value at different places in the bar graph. These cannot be compared until these are located along with other rules having similar support values. So there is a need to sort the rules in the graph based on support value. Another limitation of the visualization component is the inability to represent the confidence value. The graphical component can be enhanced by including the importance measure of interestingness of rules.

In a different approach for visualization of rules, Messaoud et al. (2007) probed into the Semiology principles. Authors worked out on an online environment for mining association rules called OLEMAR (Online Environment for Mining Association Rules). In this novel approach, authors created a complete environment for mining inter-dimensional association rules from data cubes using meta-rule guided method. These rules were validated with advanced measures called *Lift* and *Loevinger* as in the previous approach. The mining environment in this study was an enhanced version of work done by same authors in Messaoud et al. (2006). In the enhancement of previous work, authors included the support to visualize association rules. The discovered rules are presented through a visual representation based on the Graphics Semiology principles which performs rule mapping information to images. An item set is presented by a blue square and the relationship between different item sets is presented by red equilateral triangles. The support and confidence are presented by the side of the surface of shapes. Luminosity of shapes is used to define the interestingness of rules. The visualization of rules may not be much explanatory where there are many rules to compare because luminosity and surface sizes may not have clear and differentiate-able visualizations in this case.

From the techniques above, it is apparent that visualization component, if added to the mining process, can assist analysts effectively. Analysts are often interested in finding an abstract view of the results, and like the ability to dig out details further if required. As far as visualization of association rules in a multi-dimensional environment is concerned, the current approaches demonstrate some issues. The summary of these approaches is provided in the Table 4.

Firstly, the approaches which were based upon bar and ball graphs, are unable to provide a way to visualize large number of rules effectively. For ball graphs, it is not possible to show large number of rules and distinguish between these based upon support and confidence. In case of bar graphs, its not easy to distinguish different heights on a scale where large number of rules are presented having different heights in random fashion. Unless these rules are sorted by height in the graphs, the interpretation is not easy. Moreover, in some approaches only support was used to display the results, whereas other measures like confidence and importance were missed out. The techniques involving colors become ambiguous as it is not easy to interpret different shares of colors due to large number of rules. The approach which

Table 4. Visualization approaches in association rule mining over data warehouses

Authors	Title	Visualization Approach	Model	Limitations
Zhu (1998)	On-line analytical mining of association rules	Provided graphical interface to visualize rules with the help of bar and ball graphs	Data Cubes	Large number of rules is not easily distinguishable in small space.
Bogdanova and Georgieva (2005)	Discovering the association rules in OLAP data cube with daily downloads of folklore materials	Used column bar graph to show the generated rules	STAR Schema	Interpretation of larger number of rules is cumbersome in column bar graph due to similar shades of colors.
Messaoud et al. (2007)	OLEMAR: An On-Line Environment for Mining Association Rules in Multidimensional Data	Used Semiology principal based on Luminosity to show the extracted rules	STAR Schema	It is difficult to distinguish between rules due to shades of colors used in luminosity.

discussed the possibility of using Semiology Principal, although works with advanced measures called Lift and Loevinger, but it has problems with luminosity. Different shares of same color are not easy to differentiate in case of luminosity. There is a strong need of a visualization component for association rules, which resolves the issues above. In context of a strong anaylsis, such component should be interactive. To handle the issue of large number of rules, user can be asked to select the level which they want to interpret, and then rules can be represented in sets, rather than all rules at once. Since advanced measures are encouraged for mining in a data warehouse environment, such measures should be plotted in visualization component as well. So it is necessary to allow user to interpret the rules using not only Support, Confidence and Important measure, but also using measures like Lift, Loevinger, Rae, CON and Hill etc.

In this section a review of approaches has been presented which targeted pattern extraction from large data sets. These approaches involve mining over data warehouses in shape association rules. These techniques are reviewed using four parameters. The summary of these approaches is provided in the Table 5.

Firstly, it is observed that that how effectively the approaches work in environments where domain knowledge should not be a requirement for the mining process. Secondly, approaches which allowed mining at multiple levels of abstraction rather than the whole data set at once are reviewed. Thirdly, approaches have been reviewed on the basis of their evaluation criteria of generated patterns. Finally, few approaches are reviewed which provide visualization assistance to the mining process. It can be concluded that there is a strong need to provide an automated way of mining patterns without any technical and domain knowledge. It can also be concluded that mining at multiple levels is highly desired due to its ability to find patterns at different levels in the hierarchy. However, these approaches have several issues to be addressed as point above. From review of evaluation measures used for interestingness, it was found that the researchers have started targeting advanced measures for aggregate data. This area needs to be explored further. The visualization component helps out for a graphical view of the results, however the existing approaches have problems as described above. There is a need to develop a visualization component in order to provide an effective way to explore resultant rules.

Table 5. Summary of technique for association rule mining over data warehouses

Authors / Title	Model	Domain Knowledge Independent	Multi-Level Mining	Advanced Measures	Visualization
Association rule mining on data cubes Kamber et al. (1997)	Data Cubes	NO	YES	NO	NO
On-line analytical mining of association rules Zhu (1998)	Data Cubes	NO	YES	NO	YES
Hierarchy-based mining of association rules in data warehouses - Psaila and Lanzi (2000)	STAR Schema	NO	NO	NO	NO
Discovering the association rules in OLAP data cube with daily downloads of folklore materials - Bogdanova and Georgieva (2005)	Data Cubes	NO	NO	NO	YES
Enhanced mining of association rules from data cubes Messaoud et al. (2006)	Data Cubes	NO	NO	YES	NO
OLEMAR: An On-Line Environment for Mining Association Rules in Multidimensional Data - Messaoud et al. (2007)	Data Cubes	NO	NO	YES	YES
Evaluating statistical tests on OLAP cubes to compare degree of disease - Ordonez and Chen (2009)	Data Cubes	NO	NO	NO	NO
Discovering diverse association rules from multidimensional schema - Usman et al. (2013)	STAR Schema	YES	YES	YES	NO
Mining association rules from stars Wang (1999)	Data Cubes	NO	YES	NO	NO
Study on a data warehouse mining oriented fuzzy association rule mining algorithm - Wei (2014)	STAR Schema	NO	NO	NO	NO

2.2.2 Pattern Prediction From Large Datasets

As described above, pattern prediction is one of the major areas of knowledge discovery from large data sets. Prediction of patterns form large datasets remains a challenge for analysts (Sapia et al. (1999), Shazmeen, Baig, and Pawar (2013), Akinola and Oyabugbe (2015), Ristoski and Paulheim (2014)) due to the large number of dimensions and volume. Researchers have proposed techniques in past for pattern prediction over large datasets (Akinola and Oyabugbe (2015), Ristoski and Paulheim (2014), McNamara et al. (2015)). In data mining, pattern prediction is done using classification algorithm. In past, researchers have applied these algorithms on data sets to serve different purposes, which have further evolved these techniques to improve prediction accuracy, computation time and independency of domain knowledge (Brunzell and Eriksson (2000), Naeini, Moshiri, Araabi, and Sadeghi (2014), Akinola and Oyabugbe (2015)) Data warehouses have made it possible to store large volume of data for analysis purposes. Recently, large data sets are available in data warehouse environment and can be used for mining purposes. So there has been a trend to use the pattern prediction methods in multi-dimensional environment with large volume of data. Authors have acknowledged that integration of data warehouses and data mining has strengthened the knowledge discovery process and predictions over data warehouses with the help of data mining techniques are promising (Bodin-Niemczuk et al. (2008), Korikache and Yahia (2014)).

For pattern prediction, authors in past have discouraged the involvement of user in the process, as it doesn't allow the prediction of hidden interesting patterns. In these cases, since user guides the mining process, the predicted patterns generally tend to follow user's knowledge. Similarly, these techniques bound the user to have enough domain knowledge in order to predict patterns. So there has been a tendency to achieve domain knowledge independent methodologies while predicting over data warehouses (Sarawagi et al. (1998), Abdelbaki, Yahia, and Messaoud (2012), Pears, Koh, Dobbie, and Yeap (2013), Awan and Usman (2015)). Recently some techniques have emerged which involve data mining techniques in hybrid fashion. These techniques allow users to prediction patterns at multiple levels in the hierarchy rather than on the whole data set (Korikache and Yahia (2014), Awan and Usman (2015), Azeem et al. (2014)). One of the core functions of the mining process is evaluation of results. Authors have used several measures like Accuracy, Correlation Coefficient, Average Error Rate, Reduction Error, Scalability etc for evaluation purpose in past (Sair, Erraha, Elkyal, and Loudcher (2012), Korikache and Yahia (2014), Chen et al. (2006), Abdelbaki et al. (2012), Bodin-Niemczuk et al. (2008)).

2.2.2.1 Domain Knowledge Independency

As described earlier in pattern extraction section that in case where knowledge discovery is done for finding hidden patterns interesting for the users, it is important for the process to remain independent of user's domain knowledge. In these cases, the process should be automated in a way that it doesn't require a user to guide it towards interesting regions in the data sets. A review of techniques which were proposed for pattern prediction in a data warehouse environment is presented below.

Sarawagi et al. (1998) worked on guiding the user toward interesting cube regions. Their methodology employed regression model which focused on finding regions where cells had values significantly different from a threshold value. In another approach by same authors (Sarawagi (2000)), surprising information in data cube regions was found using concept of maximum entropy.

As a step towards a data mining tool integrating predictive models, data mining and data transformation to be used in medical research, Ordonez and Chen (2009) proposed to use statistical tests in order to analyze medical data sets. In order find out significant measure differences caused by some discriminating dimension, these tests are used on pairs of similar groups. In the data set used by the authors, risk factors represent the dimensions; where as the degree of disease is printed by cube measures. Authors claim that their approach is reliable for both small and large data sets. Although the results are encouraging for the authors, this approach has only be used on medical data. The main objective of authors was to assist the medical research. Therefore, they didn't not target the generalization of the approach. It is not evident as if this approach will work for variety of datasets. Secondly - in order to use these tests effectively, statistical knowledge is required for the researchers.

Abdelbaki et al. (2012) used a two step methodology to perform prediction over data cubes NAP-SC (Neural Approach for Prediction over Sparse Cubes). Although the focus of the author was to handle empty measures of the cube, but the process didn't require a user to have domain knowledge in their case for pattern prediction. Authors used Principal Component Analysis (PCA) in the pre-processing step to reduce the dimensions in the data cube. In order to convert the correlated dimension attributes into smaller sets of principal components, authors exploited the orthogonal transformation of PCA. PCA allows the authors to create PCA cubes with important dimensions which are further used in the prediction process. This methodology was tested on USA census data and appeared to be effective. However the main target of the approach was to handle sparsity that is to handle empty measures of the cube. It is not clear as if the dimension reduction used in this approach effects accuracy and computation time.

Pears et al. (2013) emphasized on the need to approaches which do not rely on user's domain knowledge for discovery of patterns. Authors state that if the methodology is dependent upon user's domain knowledge, it can incorrectly hide the hidden patterns existing in the data. Authors in this approach discovered association rules from data cubes, in which they used Principal Component Analysis (PCA) to capture the variance in each rule term. A variable having more variance can be picked over the other having low variance in this approach. The approach allows the extraction of association rules from the data cubes afterwards. The current approach is similar to this approach in terms of handling the issue of domain knowledge. However current research work intends for prediction of patterns, rather than extraction of patterns.

On similar lines for domain knowledge independent techniques, Azeem et al. (2014) presented another model for exploration of OLAP cubes via ranked paths in which, the user's domain knowledge is not required. Authors generate data cubes by picking top-ranked dimensions with the help of Principal Component Analysis (PCA). In this approach data cubes are constructed in a hierarchical level for each cluster at that level. In each cluster, variables are ranked in order to pick top ranked variables for construction of data cube. Since Pricinpal Component analysis (PCA) only works with numeric data, the authors proposed to convert nominal variables to equivalent numeric variables before PCA is applied. After conversion, PCA is applied on both numeric and nominal variables at each cluster level. Authors have tested this approach on Automobile data set. As per their results, it appears that the usage of PCA not only reduces the dimensions for cube generation, but prediction results achieved using the newly constructed data cube are better than the original data. However authors used data set called automobiles from UCI machine learning repository which doesn't contain too many variables and the number of records in this data set is also small. Therefore, this approach needs to be tested for further analysis using large datasets having large volume data and large number of dimensions.

Based on similar guidelines, Awan and Usman (2015) presented a conceptual model for prediction over OLAP cubes which also don't require the analyst to be a domain knowledge expert. This process is similar to the approach discussed before this, as it also constructs cubes at multiple levels of abstraction. To serve the objective of automatically picking the variables for cub construction, the authors proposed Multiple Correspondence Analysis (MCA) and Principal Component Analysis (PCA). Authors propose that MCA can be used for the purpose of ranking the nominal variables, and PCA can be sued to rank the numeric variables. After ranking is achieved, the cube construction can be done using these variables. Authors propose to perform prediction on data cubes using machine learning algorithms. Authors believe that adding these statistical methods for ranking of variables will only provide interesting variables for the users. However, this methodology has not been tested with the help of any data set. Since two different techniques are proposed for different types of data, the ranking process will not give correct results as during ranking it will not consider the relationship between different types of data. There is a strong need to test this methodology with some synthetic dataset in order to validate the claims.

It is apparent from the previous techniques that the domain knowledge independent techniques have gain popularity recently. To find suitable dimensions for the prediction process, the researchers in past have used different methods as summarized in Table 6. It is apparent that statistical techniques like MCA and PCA have been proposed widely in these methods. In some approaches MCA and PCA both are proposed for ranking nominal and numeric variables respectively. However, this implementation becomes ambiguous. The ranking process doesn't consider the underlying relationship existing within the different types of variables. Therefore, a single method for ranking is required. Recently, Azeem et al. (2014) developed an approach which works at multiple levels and handles this ranking issue. The proposed

Table 6. Techniques used for domain independence in prediction over data warehouses

Authors	Title	Technique Used	Limitations
Sarawagi et al. (1998)	User-Adaptive Exploration of Multidimensional Data.	Used maximum entropy to guide the user towards interesting regions in the cube.	User is involved and thus limits the possibility of hidden patterns.
Ordonez and Chen (2009)	Evaluating statistical tests on OLAP cubes to compare degree of disease.	Used statistical tests to find out significant measure differences.	Approach is not generalized.
Abdelbaki et al. (2012)	NAP-SC: a neural approach for prediction over sparse cubes.	Used Principal Component Analysis to find out interesting dimensions.	It is not clear as if the accuracy and computation time is effected using this approach.
Pears et al. (2013)	Automatic Item Weight Generation for Pattern Mining and its Application	Used Principal Component Analysis to find out interesting dimensions.	It is not clear as if only numeric data was targeted.
Azeem et al. (2014)	Intelligent data cube construction and exploration	Used Principal Component Analysis to find out interesting dimensions.	Approach is not tested on large data sets.
Awan and Usman (2015)	Intelligent analysis of data cube via statistical methods	Proposed Multiple Correspondence Analysis and Principal Component Analysis to find out interesting dimensions.	No implementation is provided for the model.

approach converts nominal variables to equivalent numeric variables and aims to apply PCA at once. This approach has only been tested on a small data set called *Automobile*, however it looks promising for large data sets.

2.2.2.2 Multi-Level Pattern Prediction

A multi-level approach allows an analyst to extract/predict patterns at multiple levels of abstraction rather than whole data at once. Approaches in literature exist, which allow users to predict patterns at multiple levels in the hierarchy. A review some techniques which work at multiple levels is presented below.

The multi-level approach was set as a future target by Sair et al. (2012) when they worked on provision of a model which was used for pattern prediction in OLAP Cubes. These OLAP cubes were generated from student's data taken from an examination management system. The authors provided prediction ability with the help of regression trees, and found that it will be interesting to implement this process at multiple levels of abstraction. Authors believed that if applied at multiple levels, their approach will produce more interesting results.

As a step towards multi-level approach, Korikache and Yahia (2014) developed a methodology that employed clustering methods. Authors presented a technique in which they divided the original data cube into sub cubes for prediction purposes. The split is done using clustering methods. For sub cube generation part, only necessary cells are used by involving a Probabilistic model which uses multinomial distribution. The authors allowed the user to select sub cube for mining process and then select the cell on which the prediction process is to be applied. Authors found that the inclusion of clustering methods allowed predicting for different clusters than for the whole dataset.

Azeem et al. (2014) presented another multi-level model for exploration of OLAP cubes via ranked paths. Their methodology involved agglomerative hierarchical clustering which allowed the authors to create clusters at multiple levels of abstraction. Authors generated data cubes at each cluster level, and explored the cubes via ranked paths. The methodology was tested on Automobiles dataset taken from UCI Machine learning repository. It was found that different results achieved at different levels in the hierarchy were interesting in nature. Although agglomerative hierarchical clustering allowed to mine at multiple levels, it has its own disadvantages. If an instance is mapped incorrectly at a lower level in a cluster, it can't be corrected in sub-sequent upper levels. Another disadvantage is the computational complexity which increases with the size of data set. So it is not suitable for large data sets. Moreover, authors used numeric variables for clustering due the Euclidean distance measure for hierarchical clustering, so methodology doesn't involve nominal variables in clustering process.

Awan and Usman (2015) presented a conceptual model for prediction over OLAP cubes. In this model data is first divided in shape of clusters at different levels in the hierarchy using agglomerative hierarchical clustering. Authors proposed to apply mining algorithms at cluster level within each hierarchical level. To achieve this, authors propose to construct data warehouse schema at cluster level and construct compact cubes. Doing this, prediction at multiple levels is possible by deploying any prediction algorithm. However, this proposed model was not tested on any dataset. Moreover, as described earlier as well, the agglomerative hierarchical clustering has some deficiencies like inability to handle an instance which was miss-classified in some iteration and increase in computational complexity with the size of data set. However, it will be interesting to replace hierarchical clustering with some more viable approach or handle the above mentioned issues while working with this clustering technique.

From the previous work in multi-level approaches for pattern prediction, it appears that authors have focused on clustering techniques as summarized in the Table 7. It has been observed generally, that researchers are interested

Table 7. Summary of multi-level mining techniques in prediction over data warehouses

Authors	Title	Multilevel Approach	Limitations
Sair et al. (2012)	Prediction in OLAP Cube	Authors proposed multi-level approach as their future endeavor.	The approach works on top level of the dataset only and is unable to predict at multiple levels.
Korikache and Yahia (2014)	Coupling OLAP and Data Mining for Prediction.	Used clustering to mining at different cluster levels.	It is not clear which clustering method has been used.
Azeem et al. (2014)	Intelligent data cube construction and exploration	Used Agglomerative Hierarchical Clustering to mine at multiple levels of abstraction in data warehouse environment	Vulnerable to the disadvantages of AHC like inability to correct miss-classification in later stages of the process.
Awan and Usman (2015)	Intelligent analysis of data cube via statistical methods	Proposed to use Agglomerative Hierarchical Clustering to mine at multiple levels of abstraction in data warehouse environment	Approach is not tested on any data set, only proposal is made.

to extract/predict patterns at multiple levels of abstraction. So it's important to have a robust method of finding levels in a large data set which is able to handle large volume of data as well as large number of dimensions. As described in above reviews, authors have used hierarchical clustering generally to achieve multiple levels. In these cases, agglomerative hierarchical cluster has been proposed or used by the authors (Azeem et al. (2014), Awan and Usman (2015)). The approach used by Azeem et al. (2014) was only tested with a small data set, which needs to be verified with a larger data set. There is a need to make the multiple levels mining more robust in order to avoid the disadvantages explained earlier.

2.2.2.3 Advanced Evaluation

Once the prediction results are available, these must be validated and evaluated using some measures. In past, measures like accuracy, scalability etc were used for measure the classification ability of a particular algorithm or a technique. However, recently few more measures like Recall, Precision, F-Measure etc have been introduced and are being used in validation process of a general classification method. Same measures can be used to evaluate and validate a predictive model in a multi-dimensional environment. In this sub-section, a review of some techniques which targeted evaluation of predicted patterns from data warehouses is presented.

In order to evaluate their predicted patterns, Ordonez and Chen (2009) used computation time, scalability and efficiency measures. Authors designed an approach for prediction over data cubes in which they created prediction cubes using general data cubes in which each cell is computed by evaluating the model built on the data sub set defined by the cell instead of using simple aggregate measures like sum and average. The authors provided decomposable scoring functions for well known algorithms like J48, KB, and Naïve Bayes algorithms. The evaluation of this technique has been done on 8 data sets (adult, kr-vs-kp, nursery,pendigits, satimage, spambase, waveform, and letter) taken from UCI machine learning website. Accuracy measure for classification in all these datasets is obtained by creating data cubes as per their methodology. Authors have shown the as the data set size gets larger, the accuracy remains almost same on a linear curve. The technique is also evaluated using computation time, scalability and efficiency measures apart from the general accuracy measure. However advanced measures like Recall, Precision and F-Measure are not tested.

In a similar approach, targeting the computation time, Chen et al. (2006) worked in multi-dimensional environment for predictions using regression techniques. Authors proposed the concept of regression cubes and a data cell compression technique NCR (nonlinear compression representation) to support efficient OLAP operations in the regression cubes. Such compression appeared to save computation time and space in Stream Cube environment. The methodology has been tested on two synthetic data sets, and experiments show efficiency in terms of computation time and space. The computation time and space consumption is small in comparison to the exhaustive methods. However, this study is limited to the numeric data as per information provided by the authors. Moreover, measures like accuracy, recall, Precision, and F-Measures were not evaluated.

In order to handle the issue of nominal/categorical data, Xi, Lin, and Chen (2009) provided an approached based on logistic regression prediction in a multi-dimensional environment. The method adapted by the authors performs compression on data cells to quickly perform operations. The main target of the methodology was to save the computation time and space. The methodology loses little amount of accuracy as a cost of saving computation time and space required for the mining process. This approach is tested on two synthetic datasets and appears to be effective. Authors have shown the computation time and space requirements decrease in their methodology. However, the accuracy in this case is degraded to a very small level. However, this approach only works for categorical type of data since its based on a logistic regression. Moreover, authors didn't provide any evaluation using advanced measures like Precision, Recall and F-Measure. It will be interesting to see if Precision, Recall and F-Measures are also not compromised a lot like accuracy while saving computation time and space using the provided approach.

Another approach targeting the evaluation using average error rate and error reduction was proposed by Bodin-Niemczuk et al. (2008). In their methodology authors used regression trees for prediction in a multidimensional environment. Authors found that coupling of OLAP with Data mining techniques have the potential towards pattern prediction. Authors used Automatic Interaction Detection (AID) learning algorithm to build the regression tree. For testing purposes, authors used the approach on a medical data set. The approach utilized 70% of the data for training and 30% of the data for testing purposes. The approach appeared to be effective with the usage of regression trees as evaluated by error rate and error reduction measures. Although regression trees work better than some other algorithms where high number of dimensions is involved, however, these are unstable in nature as small change in the data results in a completely different tree. Secondly, the authors didn't test this approach on any other data set apart from the medical data set used in testing. It will be interesting to see the effectiveness of this methodology on variety of data sets. Moreover, authors didn't provide evaluation using advanced measures like Recall, Precision and F-Measure.

Another approach that used average error rate and reduction error as a measure for evaluation was developed by Sair et al. (2012). The authors used regression trees for pattern prediction over data warehouses mainly targeting the context-based analysis. In the approach presented by the authors, validation was done by using students data. 1200 facts were present in the data cube used in the study and it was taken from an examination management system. Authors used 70% of the data to train the model, where as 30% data was used for testing purposes. It was found that average error rate and reduction error rates were within the required ranges and were acceptable. These results were not compared with any other model, as well as no other measure like Recall, Precision or F-Measure was used. The approach becomes limited as well, because it was not tested on any synthetic data set apart from the data specific to the examination management system used by the authors. It will be interesting to see the effectiveness of this approach on variety of data sets, as well as the evaluation with other measures like Recall, Precision and F-Measure.

Similar to the above approach, Korikache and Yahia (2014) used error rate and error reduction measures for evaluating their results in their prediction mode. Authors presented a technique in which they divided the original data cube into sub cubes for prediction purposes. After generation of sub cubes, authors used regression trees. The implementation of the model was performed by taking 70% data for learning and 30% for testing. The authors used measures like average error rate and error reduction for evaluation purposes. It appeared that approach was effective based on these two measures and provides acceptable results, however, advanced measures such as Recall, Precision and F-Measure are not calculated. It will be interesting to see the effectiveness of their approach with these advanced measures of interestingness. Secondly, authors used a single data set to validate their model, so there is a requirement to check this approach on variety of data sets

Different from the above few approaches, Abdelbaki et al. (2012) validated their model using accuracy and correlation coefficient measures. The authors proposed a two step methodology to perform prediction over data cubes. The focus of the authors was to handle the empty measures of the cube. They coupled machine learning and statistical methods for pattern prediction. For predictions over data cubes, the authors used MLP (Multilayer Perception) algorithm. The authors used 70% of the data for training purposes and 30% of the data for testing purposes. The model has been tested on USA census data. The approach handles the sparsity effectively as shown in the experiments. The authors have used Accuracy and Correlation Coefficient measures for evaluation of their results. The approach has been reported to be effective with these measures, however, they major concern was to deal with the sparsity issue. The authors didn't test the approach on variety of data sets as well as they didn't use advanced measures like Recall, Precision and F-Measure etc.

From the above approaches, it appears the authors have targeted the evaluation of predictive patterns in mining process as summarized in the Table 8. Some approaches exist which targeted accuracy, scalability and efficiency (Chen et al. (2005)) by creating cubes specifically for prediction purposes. Another category of approaches focus on evaluation of predicted patterns generated from regression trees. In these cases, some approaches deal with

Table 8. Summary of evaluation techniques in prediction over data warehouses

Authors	Title	Evaluation Measures	Limitations
Ordonez and Chen (2009)	Prediction cubes	Proposed the concept of prediction cubes and compared accuracy, scalability, efficiency and computation time with exhaustive methods.	Didn't evaluate the model using advanced measures like Recall, Precision and F-Measure.
Xi et al. (2009)	Compression and aggregation for logistic regression analysis in data cubes.	Provided prediction of categorical data using logistic regression, and reduced time and space requirements.	Accuracy is compromised a little. Only works with categorical data. Measures like Recall, Precision, F-Measure are not evaluated.
Chen et al. (2006)	Regression cubes with lossless compression and aggregation.	Proposed compression measure in regression cubes. Saves Computation time and space.	Approach is only applicable to numeric data. Measures like Accuracy, Recall, Precision, F-Measure are not checked.
Bodin-Niemczuk et al. (2008)	Towards the integration of prediction in OLAP cubes	Evaluated the model using error rate and error reduction measures for regression trees.	Model is only tested on medical data set. The approach is not evaluated using Accuracy, Recall, Precision and F-Measures.
Korikache and Yahia (2014)	Coupling OLAP and Data Mining for Prediction.	Evaluated the model using error rate and error reduction measures for regression trees.	Model is only tested on a single data set. The approach is not evaluated using Accuracy, Recall, Precision and F-Measures.
Sair et al. (2012)	Prediction in OLAP Cubes	Evaluated the model using error rate and error reduction measures for regression trees.	Model is only tested on a single data set. The approach is not evaluated using Accuracy, Recall, Precision and F-Measures.
Abdelbaki et al. (2012)	NAP-SC: a neural approach for prediction over sparse cubes.	Validated the model using Accuracy and Correlation Coefficients.	Didn't evaluate the model using advanced measures like Recall, Precision and F-Measure

only numeric data, and some only deal with the nominal data. Secondly, these approaches are not well-tesed on synthetic data sets. (Xi et al. (2009), Chen et al. (2006), Bodin-Niemczuk et al. (2008), Korikache and Yahia (2014)). Moreover, in these approaches, no author focused on evaluating the model using advanced measures like Recall, Precision and F-Measure. The target remained to validate the model using average error rate and error reduction measures. The approach presented by Abdelbaki et al. (2012)) evaluates the model using accuracy and correlation coefficient, but it is more focused on handling sparsity. Authors didn't focus on advanced measures apart from accuracy and correlation coefficient. From the review of these approaches, it is evident that there is a strong need to use advanced criteria for evaluation of model while working in pattern prediction techniques over data warehouses. Measures like Accuracy, Recall, Precision and F-Measure are more suited for aggregate data in data warehouse environment.

In this section a review of the approaches which targeted pattern prediction from large data sets is presented. Different approaches have been proposed in past for pattern prediction from data warehouses using data mining techniques. These approaches are reviewed using three parameters like in the case of pattern extraction. A summary of these approaches is given in the Table 9. First the approaches are explored in the context of domain independency. It is found that not all approaches provide domain independency due to the fact that these involve user in the mining process. The method becomes user-drive in these cases, and therefore doesn't look for hidden patterns. There are some approaches which are able to automate the process of knowledge discovery without human intervention with the help of statistical methods like PCA and MCA etc. (Abdelbaki et al. (2012), Azeem et al. (2014), Awan and Usman (2015)). First two approaches are not well-tested on synthetic dataset, however these look promising. The third approach in the list, has not been implemented yet. However, the authors have proposed to rank variables using two different approaches which become ambiguous. If two methods are used separately, the relationship between these both types of variables is not considered. So there is a need to create a robust method which is able to work with both types of data in error free manner. Secondly, these approaches are reviewed in terms of their ability to mine at multiple levels of abstraction. Most approaches work on a single level, but recently few authors have started working with multiple levels. In this area, hierarchical clustering has been used mostly. However it only works with numeric data. Moreover, as detailed before, if an instance is miss-classified at a lower stage, it cannot be corrected in later stages. Thirdly, it is found that no approach utilizes advanced measures of

Table 9. Summary of Techniques used for prediction over data warehouses

Authors / Title	No. of Datasets Used	Domain Knowledge Independency	Multi-Level Mining	Advanced Evaluation
User-Adaptive Exploration of Multidimensional Data Sarawagi et al. (1998)	1	NO	NO	NO
Prediction cubes Chen et al. (2005)	8	NO	NO	NO
Regression cubes with lossless compression and Aggregation - Chen et al. (2006)	2	NO	NO	NO
Towards the integration of prediction in OLAP cubes Bodin-Niemczuk et al. (2008)	1	NO	NO	NO
Compression and aggregation for logistic regression analysis in data cubes. - Xi et al. (2009)	1	NO	NO	NO
Evaluating statistical tests on OLAP cubes to compare degree of disease. -	1	NO	NO	NO
Prediction in OLAP Cubes Sair et al. (2012)	1	NO	NO	NO
NAP-SC: a neural approach for prediction over sparse cubes. Abdelbaki et al. (2012)	1	YES	NO	NO
Automatic Item Weight Generation for Pattern Mining and its Application - Pears et al. (2013)	1	YES	NO	NO
Coupling OLAP and Data Mining for Prediction Korikache and Yahia (2014)	1	NO	YES	NO
Intelligent data cube construction and exploration Azeem et al. (2014)	1	YES	YES	NO
Intelligent analysis of data cube via statistical methods Awan and Usman (2015)	0	YES	YES	NO

interestingness like Recall, Precision and F-Measure. There is a need to apply these measures while predicting patterns over data warehouses.

2.3 EMERGING RESEARCH AND OPPORTUNITIES

In this section we review some of the recent research being done in the area of pattern extraction and prediction in large data sets.

In a recent study (Cuzzocrea, 2017), two proposals are presented to show the usage of data mining techniques on social data. First method is provided to support OLAP analysis over multidimensional tweet streams. Authors provide real world case study on tweets associated to the 2015 campaign of Italian Election. The data is taken from Twitter API dealing with public tweets. Data is collected and imported into the data warehouse created for OLAP analysis. Wikify (a wikification service) is used to recognize the sense of main topic of the tweet in order to assign the weight to that tweet. The Meta data of tweets helps to define the dimension of data in the OLAP cubes, which are further explored using OLAP techniques. The other method uses multidimensional clustering methods to support analysis over geo-tagged data. One component of this methodology is called FollowMe Suite which discovers posts shared by the travelers discover from locations. Another component called Trip Analysis Suite creates clusters of trips which are shown on a web portal. It is not clear which clustering method is used for clustering the data. It will be interesting to check the effectiveness of both methodologies using different types of data warehouses and clustering methods.

In another recent study (Yuan, 2017), authors have presented a new algorithm called T-Apriori. The study focuses on two major issues of Apriori Algorithm that is, scanning of whole data set frequently and large number of candidate sets. Another version of Algorithm is presented which creates a new mapping way in order to avoid scanning of datasets, improves joining efficiency and achieves high efficiency using an overlap strategy to count support. The new algorithm is defined as T-Apriori Algorithm. The results of this algorithm are compared with Apriori Algorithm, Bitxor and I-Apriori algorithms. A case study on Mushrooms dataset has been done to show the improvements in time consumption up to 98%. However it is not tested on variety of large datasets and thus not generalized. The space complexity has also not been compared with the other approaches.

In order to utilize Association Rule Mining and OLAP, authors in (Jeon et al., 2017) have proposed a technique for rule-based topic trend analysis on social data. The analysis is conducted by combining On-Line-Analytical Processing (OLAP) with Association Rule Mining (ARM). The data in this methodology is collected from twitter for testing purposes. The model first removes un-necessary words from the data. In second step LDA is applied to extract topics from the data. A multi-dimensional STAR schema is generated and data is imported into the data warehouse. Afterwards Association Rule Mining is applied to extract patterns from the aggregate data. However the interestingness is measured using conventional measures like Support and Confidence. Morever, the schema creates only one Fact variable which limits the analysis as there can multiple Fact variables in a real data set.

More Recently authors in (Hahsler & Karpienko, 2017) have designed a new technique for visualization of association rules. Authors explained that the existing techniques of visualization of association rules are not capable of handling large number of association rules. Techniques like scatter plots, double-decker plots, parallel plots have been used, however these techniques are not suitable for displaying the large sets of rules. Authors have introduced a new method called grouped matrix-based visualization which creates groups of rules using clustering. The clusters of rules can further be explored up to an individual rule. The rules are presented in a plot format where colors and positioning of elements defines the interestingness of rules. However, it is not clear which interestingness measure is used to filter the rules. The implementation of this methodology is done on a sample dataset, and authors seek to implement this methodology on a large data set. The methodology is implemented in R-Language and requires technical knowledge for business analysts to explore the rules.

In another recent work, authors in Ramírez-Gallego, Krawczyk, García, Woźniak, and Herrera (2017) provided a review of pre processing techniques for the data taken from data streams for mining purposes. Authors have conducted an analysis of methods used in this regard based upon their computational time, reduction rates, predictive performance, and memory usage. 20 datasets have been used in this research work for analysis purposes where 7 out of these data sets were generated artificially. Feature selection yields better results using Naive Bayes method as compared to Information Gain, SU and OFS algorithms in terms of accuracy. Authors have further analyzed CPU Usage and Memory Usage of these algorithms. However, authors state that the data pre-processing of data streams is still in early phases. Discretization remains one of the major tasks in future in this area.

2.4 ISSUES IN CURRENT RESEARCH

In this section, a review of the current research is presented in terms of different parameters to identify certain gaps. The parameters include domain knowledge independence, multi-level mining, advanced evaluation and visualization as discussed by (Han et al., 2011).

2.4.1 Issues in Pattern Extraction

As described in the previous sections recent research has focused on mining from data warehousing by either using data cubes or by exploiting the STAR Schema. Although researchers are able to extract informative hidden patterns in the form of association rules, some issues require attention.

Firstly, techniques in past focus on mining at multiple levels by generating data warehouse schema with top-ranked dimensions. Involvement of user with domain knowledge is not a requirement in this case. Most of the techniques are able to reduce the number of dimensions; however such techniques result in removing dimensions which have hidden interesting patterns. One of the techniques doesn't involve user in the feature selection process, but it ranks numeric and nominal data separately. The inter-relation between different types of data is not considered while ranking is done. There is a need to adapt a procedure which can rank both types of data at the same time. By ranking variables at the same time, the relationship within the data is not lost. This way, top ranked variables from whole data set are picked strengthening the ranking process.

Secondly, researchers in past have not worked at multiple levels of abstraction in most cases. Usman et al. (2013) has adapted a multi-level approach to mine STAR schema which shows that it is worth mining at multiple levels for business analysts. The schema is generated at cluster level within levels of hierarchy. This process remains cumbersome while mining a large data set, since it has to work at each cluster level to create a schema for mining. Therefore, it is proposed that an automation of schema generation process will strengthen the technique.

Thirdly, the evaluation of association rules generated through these techniques is majorly achieved using conventional measures like Count, Support and Confidence. These measures were designed to work with the transactional databases only. Researchers have proposed some advanced measures in particular for mining in a data warehouse environment. These measures are based on aggregate data, and thus are more meaningful that the conventional measures. Therefore, there is a strong requirement to evaluate the pattern extraction models using advanced measures like Rae, Con, Hill, Lift and Loevinger etc. Moreover, if this process is done at multiple levels of abstraction like in the case of Usman et al. (2013), it becomes cumbersome. The calculation of these measures at every cluster level within each level will not be easy. Therefore, it is recommended automating this process of calculation of advance measures at multiple levels.

Finally, for visualization, it is observed that most techniques do not provide visualization whereas it is a helpful addition to the mining process. Some of the techniques however provide this support but at the same time, these are sensitive to large number of rules. Most of these techniques are although able to display the rules in small available space in the interface, but these are not interpretable. Authors have used Ball and Bar Graphs mostly, and it is not easy to distinguish between width and height of balls and bars respectively where researcher has a large resultant set of rules. The approaches which use shades of colors to distinguish rules are also troublesome. It is not easy to differentiate between same shades, as more shades will be used when more rules are generated. Another issue in these techniques is the inability to provide support for showing rules satisfying advanced measures, as most of these only focus support and confidence filters. Therefore, there is a need of visualization component that not only provides ability to show large number of rules in a small space, but also allows researchers to dig out rules using advance measure filters like importance, Rae, Con and Hill etc.

2.4.2 Issues in Pattern Prediction

As described in the previous section that recent research has focused on prediction from data warehousing by deploying classification algorithms. Although researchers are able to predict informative hidden patterns, some issues require attention.

It is evident from the previous techniques that the domain knowledge independent techniques have gain popularity recently. To find suitable dimensions for the prediction process, the researchers in past have used different methods. Some techniques work only for numeric data utilizing algorithms working with the numeric only. Similarly, there are some techniques which only work on nominal or categorical data. There is another category of techniques which handle both nominal and numeric data. A prediction model should support predictions for both types of data available in all domains. However, the existing techniques which work specifically for this purpose have issues. In one of the available technique, the ranking of variables is used to pick the variables for prediction purposes. This ranking procedure although works for both types of variables, but it ranks both variables separately and doesn't take the relationship that exists in the data. The ranking process becomes ambiguous in such cases. There is a strong need of a technique that works for both types of data effectively.

Secondly, there has been a trend to apply pattern prediction at multiple levels of abstraction. It certainly allows one to predict patterns at multiple levels than on top of a whole dataset. However, not many techniques exist in this regard when mining in data warehouse. One of the techniques involving hierarchical clustering attempts to work at multiple levels. It looks promising as the results given by the authors are different at different levels, as different predictions are made at each level. However, it has not been tested on a large data set to check its effectiveness. Usually data in a data warehouse environment is in large quantity and also involves large number of dimensions. Since mining at multiple levels has many advantages, it is worth to check this technique for larger data sets which involves large volume of data and large number of dimensions.

Finally, almost all approaches didn't use advanced measures of evaluation of prediction results. The researchers have focused on measures accuracy, correlation coefficient, computation time and space measures. The advanced measures like Recall, Precision and F-Measures must be checked as these measures are more suited to work with multi-dimensional environment. Moreover, in most of the cases, the models are tested in specific domains as the target was to achieve certain capabilities within specific areas like prediction of disease or software error detection. Therefore, there is a requirement to test the models on a variety of data sets. More importantly, the validation should be performed on the datasets having large number of records and dimensions as data volume in data warehouses is normally large.

2.5 RESEARCH OBJECTIVES AND PLAN FOR MULTI-LEVEL PATTERN EXTRACTION AND PREDICTION

In the previous section the issues in existing techniques of pattern extraction and pattern prediction in large data sets have been discussed. There is a strong need for a methodology that has ability to resolve the above mentioned issues.

The aim of this research work is to design a methodology which can work on multiple levels of abstraction, and has the ability to extract and predict patterns. It is aimed that the model is not dependent on the domain and technical knowledge of the user. It is also aimed that evaluation of extraction and prediction model is done with the help of advanced measures. Moreover, the research intends to provide visualization support of extracted patterns. To serve these purposes, the model targets to mine at multiple levels of abstraction like Usman et al. (2013) using hierarchical clustering. For pattern extraction as well as to build prediction model, effective dimension reduction techniques are proposed to automatically pick variables for mining process. This step enables the model to remove the requirement of domain knowledge for business analysts. Usman et al. (2013) is able to resolve the issue of domain knowledge requirement but their technique has issues in the ranking process. It ranks both numeric and nominal types of data separately. This research intends to use a single method for ranking of both nominal and numeric variables to resolve this issue. To achieve this nominal variables are converted to equivalent numeric variables. After the conversion, Principal Component Analysis is proposed to pick top ranked variables. These variables are used in the generation of data warehouse schema at each cluster level. The model also intends to automate the process of data warehouse schema generation at each level of hierarchy to reduce the manual effort. Furthermore, conventional *Apriori* algorithm is applied at each cluster level to mine association rules and evaluate these using diversity measures called Rae, CON, Hill instead of using conventional measures. The model also plans to automate the diversity calculation process to reduce time required for calculation. For pattern prediction, the research work aims to build classification models at multiple levels of abstraction as it appears to be effective for business analysts. In this case the model generates clusters using hierarchical clustering like before and then picks top ranked variables using Normality Measure. A variable which better satisfies the normal distribution can be picked over the other in ranking process. Afterwards different classification algorithms are aimed to apply at each cluster level to build the classification model. By application of multiple algorithms, model aims to find accuracy, recall, precision and f-measures of these algorithms and draw a comparison of these. The model also aims to compare the time required for building the model at each cluster level for all algorithms. After these measures are calculated, a visualization component is proposed to visualize these results and model selection. The selected model is then proposed to use for pattern predictions.

2.6 CONCLUSION

In this section literature review of techniques available covering knowledge discovery has been presented. These techniques involve knowledge discovery in shape of pattern extraction and pattern prediction in a data warehouse environment. The available literature suggests that there are a number of issues in the techniques available for patter extraction as well as pattern prediction approaches. The review also describes the issues in both areas explicitly. By the end of the section, the key target areas of this research have been discussed. The next chapter discusses the proposed model for pattern extraction and pattern prediction from large data sets.

REFERENCES

Abdelbaki, W., Yahia, S. B., & Messaoud, R. B. (2012). *NAP-SC: a neural approach for prediction over sparse cubes.* Paper presented at the International Conference on Advanced Data Mining and Applications. doi:10.1007/978-3-642-35527-1_29

Agrawal, R., Imielinski, T., & Swami, A. (1993). Mining Associations between Sets of Items in Massive Databases. *Proceedings of the ACM-SIGMOD Int'l Conference on Management of Data.*

Akinola, S. O., & Oyabugbe, O. J. (2015). Accuracies and Training Times of Data Mining Classification Algorithms: An Empirical Comparative Study. *Journal of Software Engineering and Applications, 8*(9), 470–477. doi:10.4236/jsea.2015.89045

Awan, M. M., & Usman, M. (2015). *Intelligent analysis of data cube via statistical methods.* Paper presented at the Digital Information Management (ICDIM), 2015 Tenth International Conference on. doi:10.1109/ICDIM.2015.7381880

Azeem, M., Usman, M., & Ahmad, W. (2014). *Intelligent data cube construction and exploration.* Paper presented at the Digital Information Management (ICDIM), 2014 Ninth International Conference on. doi:10.1109/ICDIM.2014.6991408

Berson, A., & Smith, S. J. (1997). *Data warehousing, data mining, and OLAP.* McGraw-Hill, Inc.

Bodin-Niemczuk, A., Messaoud, R. B., Rabaséda, S. L., & Boussaid, O. (2008). Vers l'intégration de la prédiction dans les cubes OLAP. *Et gestion des connaissances: EGC'2008.*

Bogdanova, G., & Georgieva, T. (2005). *Discovering the association rules in OLAP data cube with daily downloads of folklore materials.* Paper presented at the International Conference on Computer Systems and Technologies.

Brunzell, H., & Eriksson, J. (2000). Feature reduction for classification of multidimensional data. *Pattern Recognition, 33*(10), 1741–1748. doi:10.1016/S0031-3203(99)00142-9

Castillo-Rojas, W., Vargas, C., & Villegas, C. M. (2014). Interactive Visualization of Association Rules Model Using SOM. *Proceedings of the XV International Conference on Human Computer Interaction.* doi:10.1145/2662253.2691319

Chaudhuri, S., & Dayal, U. (1997). An overview of data warehousing and OLAP technology. *SIGMOD Record, 26*(1), 65–74. doi:10.1145/248603.248616

Chen, Y., Dong, G., Han, J., Pei, J., Wah, B. W., & Wang, J. (2006). Regression cubes with lossless compression and aggregation. *IEEE Transactions on Knowledge and Data Engineering, 18*(12), 1585–1599. doi:10.1109/TKDE.2006.196

Cios, K. J., Pedrycz, W., & Swiniarski, R. W. (1998). *Data Mining and Knowledge Discovery. In Data Mining Methods for Knowledge Discovery* (pp. 1–26). Springer. doi:10.1007/978-1-4615-5589-6

Cuzzocrea, A. (2017). *Multidimensional mining of big social data for supporting advanced big data analytics.* Paper presented at the Information and Communication Technology, Electronics and Microelectronics (MIPRO), 2017 40th International Convention on. doi:10.23919/MIPRO.2017.7973630

Dong, G., & Li, J. (1999). Efficient mining of emerging patterns: Discovering trends and differences. *Proceedings of the fifth ACM SIGKDD international conference on Knowledge discovery and data mining.* doi:10.1145/312129.312191

Fayyad, U., Piatetsky-Shapiro, G., & Smyth, P. (1996). From data mining to knowledge discovery in databases. *AI Magazine, 17*(3), 37.

Frawley, W. J., Piatetsky-Shapiro, G., & Matheus, C. J. (1992). Knowledge discovery in databases: An overview. *AI Magazine, 13*(3), 57.

Goebel, M., & Gruenwald, L. (1999). A survey of data mining and knowledge discovery software tools. *ACM SIGKDD Explorations Newsletter, 1*(1), 20-33.

Hahsler, M., & Karpienko, R. (2017). Visualizing association rules in hierarchical groups. *Journal of Business Economics*, *87*(3), 317–335. doi:10.1007/s11573-016-0822-8

Han, J., Kamber, M., & Chiang, J. (1997). *Mining Multi-Dimensional Association Rules Using Data Cubes: Technical report*. Database Systems Research Laboratory, School of Science, Simon Fraser University.

Han, J., Pei, J., & Kamber, M. (2011). *Data mining: concepts and techniques*. Elsevier.

Hand, D. J., Mannila, H., & Smyth, P. (2001). *Principles of data mining*. MIT Press.

Hipp, J., Güntzer, U., & Nakhaeizadeh, G. (2000). Algorithms for association rule mining—a general survey and comparison. *ACM SIGKDD Explorations Newsletter, 2*(1), 58-64.

Hsu, S.-C., & Chien, C.-F. (2007). Hybrid data mining approach for pattern extraction from wafer bin map to improve yield in semiconductor manufacturing. *International Journal of Production Economics*, *107*(1), 88–103. doi:10.1016/j.ijpe.2006.05.015

Jeon, Y., Cho, C., Seo, J., Kwon, K., Park, H., & Chung, I.-J. (2017). *Rule-Based Topic Trend Analysis by Using Data Mining Techniques. In Advanced Multimedia and Ubiquitous Engineering* (pp. 466–473). Springer.

Kamber, M., Han, J., & Chiang, J. (1997). *Metarule-Guided Mining of Multi-Dimensional Association Rules Using Data Cubes*. Paper presented at the KDD.

Kimball, R., & Caserta, J. (2011). *The Data Warehouse ETL Toolkit: Practical Techniques for Extracting, Cleaning, Conforming, and Delivering Data*. John Wiley & Sons.

Korikache, N., & Yahia, A. (2014). *Coupling OLAP and Data Mining for Prediction*. Academic Press.

Liu, G., Suchitra, A., Zhang, H., Feng, M., Ng, S.-K., & Wong, L. (2012). AssocExplorer: an association rule visualization system for exploratory data analysis. *Proceedings of the 18th ACM SIGKDD international conference on Knowledge discovery and data mining*. doi:10.1145/2339530.2339774

Liu, Z., & Guo, M. (2001). *A proposal of integrating data mining and on-line analytical processing in data warehouse.* Paper presented at the Info-tech and Info-net, 2001. Proceedings. ICII 2001-Beijing. 2001 International Conferences on. doi:10.1109/ICII.2001.983049

McNamara, D. S., Crossley, S. A., Roscoe, R. D., Allen, L. K., & Dai, J. (2015). A hierarchical classification approach to automated essay scoring. *Assessing Writing, 23*, 35–59. doi:10.1016/j.asw.2014.09.002

Messaoud, R. B., Rabaséda, S. L., Boussaid, O., & Missaoui, R. (2006). Enhanced mining of association rules from data cubes. *Proceedings of the 9th ACM international workshop on Data warehousing and OLAP.* doi:10.1145/1183512.1183517

Messaoud, R. B., Rabaséda, S. L., Rokia, M., & Boussaid, O. (2007). OLEMAR: an online environment for mining association rules in multidimensional data. *Data Mining and Knowledge Discovery Technologies, 35.*

Naeini, M. P., Moshiri, B., Araabi, B. N., & Sadeghi, M. (2014). Learning by abstraction: Hierarchical classification model using evidential theoretic approach and Bayesian ensemble model. *Neurocomputing, 130,* 73–82. doi:10.1016/j.neucom.2012.03.041

Ordonez, C., & Chen, Z. (2009). Evaluating statistical tests on OLAP cubes to compare degree of disease. *IEEE Transactions on Information Technology in Biomedicine, 13*(5), 756–765. doi:10.1109/TITB.2008.926989 PMID:19273013

Palpanas, T. (2000). Knowledge discovery in data warehouses. *SIGMOD Record, 29*(3), 88–100. doi:10.1145/362084.362142

Pears, R., Koh, Y. S., Dobbie, G., & Yeap, W. (2013). Weighted association rule mining via a graph based connectivity model. *Information Sciences, 218,* 61–84. doi:10.1016/j.ins.2012.07.001

Psaila, G., & Lanzi, P. L. (2000). Hierarchy-based mining of association rules in data warehouses. *Proceedings of the 2000 ACM symposium on Applied computing, 1.* doi:10.1145/335603.335773

Ramírez-Gallego, S., Krawczyk, B., García, S., Woźniak, M., & Herrera, F. (2017). A survey on data preprocessing for data stream mining: Current status and future directions. *Neurocomputing, 239,* 39–57. doi:10.1016/j.neucom.2017.01.078

Ristoski, P., & Paulheim, H. (2014). *Feature selection in hierarchical feature spaces.* Paper presented at the International Conference on Discovery Science.

Sair, A., Erraha, B., Elkyal, M., & Loudcher, S. (2012). Prediction in OLAP Cube. *IJCSI International Journal of Computer Science Issues, 9*(4), 449–458.

Sapia, C., Höfling, G., Müller, M., Hausdorf, C., Stoyan, H., & Grimmer, U. (1999). *On supporting the data warehouse design by data mining techniques.* Paper presented at the Proc. GI-Workshop Data Mining and Data Warehousing.

Sarawagi, S. (2000). *User-Adaptive Exploration of Multidimensional Data.* Paper presented at the VLDB.

Sarawagi, S., Agrawal, R., & Megiddo, N. (1998). *Discovery-driven exploration of OLAP data cubes.* Paper presented at the International Conference on Extending Database Technology.

Sekhavat, Y. A., & Hoeber, O. (2013). *Visualizing association rules using linked matrix, graph, and detail views.* Academic Press.

Shazmeen, S. F., Baig, M. M. A., & Pawar, M. R. (2013). Performance Evaluation of Different Data Mining Classification Algorithm and Predictive Analysis. *Journal of Computer Engineering, 10*(6), 1-6.

Song, I.-Y., Khare, R., An, Y., Lee, S., Kim, S.-P., Kim, J., & Moon, Y.-S. (2008). *SAMSTAR: An automatic tool for generating star schemas from an entity-relationship diagram.* Paper presented at the International Conference on Conceptual Modeling. doi:10.1007/978-3-540-87877-3_42

Usman, M., Asghar, S., & Fong, S. (2009). *A conceptual model for combining enhanced olap and data mining systems.* Paper presented at the INC, IMS and IDC, 2009. NCM'09. Fifth International Joint Conference on. doi:10.1109/NCM.2009.354

Usman, M., Pears, R., & Fong, A. C. M. (2013). Discovering diverse association rules from multidimensional schema. *Expert Systems with Applications, 40*(15), 5975–5996. doi:10.1016/j.eswa.2013.05.031

Wang, X. Z. (1999). *Data Mining and Knowledge Discovery—an Overview. In Data Mining and Knowledge Discovery for Process Monitoring and Control* (pp. 13–28). Springer. doi:10.1007/978-1-4471-0421-6_2

Wei, H. (2014). *Study on a data warehouse mining oriented fuzzy association rule mining algorithm.* Paper presented at the Intelligent Systems Design and Engineering Applications (ISDEA), 2014 Fifth International Conference on. doi:10.1109/ISDEA.2014.207

Wu, X., Zhu, X., Wu, G.-Q., & Ding, W. (2014). Data mining with big data. *IEEE Transactions on Knowledge and Data Engineering, 26*(1), 97–107. doi:10.1109/TKDE.2013.109

Xi, R., Lin, N., & Chen, Y. (2009). Compression and aggregation for logistic regression analysis in data cubes. *IEEE Transactions on Knowledge and Data Engineering, 21*(4), 479–492. doi:10.1109/TKDE.2008.186

Yadav, D., & Pal, S. (2015). An Integration of Clustering and Classification Technique in Software Error Detection. *African Journal of Computing and ICT, 8*(2).

You, J., Dillon, T., & Liu, J. (2001). *An integration of data mining and data warehousing for hierarchical multimedia information retrieval.* Paper presented at the Intelligent Multimedia, Video and Speech Processing. doi:10.1109/ISIMP.2001.925411

Yuan, X. (2017). *An improved Apriori algorithm for mining association rules.* Paper presented at the AIP Conference. doi:10.1063/1.4977361

Zbidi, N., Faiz, S., & Limam, M. (2006). On mining summaries by objective measures of interestingness. *Machine Learning, 62*(3), 175–198. doi:10.1007/s10994-005-5066-8

Zhu, H. (1998). *On-line analytical mining of association rules.* Simon Fraser University.

Chapter 3
Conceptual Model for Predictive Analysis on Large Data

ABSTRACT

This chapter provides an overview of the proposed model for pattern extraction and pattern prediction over data warehouses. As discussed before, the main objective of the research is to provide a single model for pattern extraction and prediction. The objectives include an automated way to select variables for the mining process, automated schema design, advanced evaluation of extracted patterns, and visualization of extracted patterns.

3.1 PROPOSED METHODOLOGY: FRAMEWORK AND DATASET INTRODUCTION

Figure 1 shows the model showing different phases involved in the model. The extraction and prediction of patterns is shown by using different paths. The extraction of patterns is shown through path E in the figure. The prediction of patterns is done through Path P1, P2 and P3 depending upon the nature of variables being used for prediction and the nature of variables being predicted.

Path E in the Figure 1 contains steps to extract patterns. The steps involve generation of clusters, ranking of variables, multidimensional scaling, STAR schema generation, mining of association rules, evaluation using advanced measures and visualization of association rules. Pattern prediction is done

DOI: 10.4018/978-1-5225-5029-7.ch003

Figure 1. Model for multi-level pattern extraction and pattern prediction

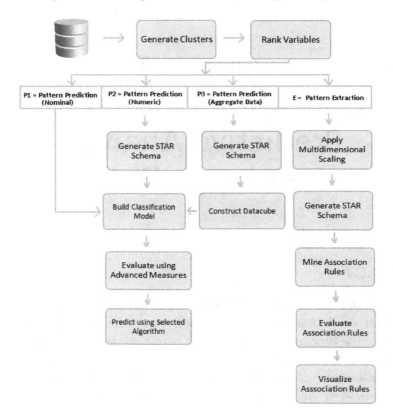

using paths P1, P2, and P3. Path P1 in the figure contains steps to predict nominal variables. This path involves generation of clusters, ranking of variables, building of classification model, evaluation of models, selection of model and prediction using the selected model. Path P2 in the figure shows the steps to predict numeric variables. The involved steps are generation of clusters, ranking of variables, STAR schema generation, classification model building, evaluation of models, selection of model and prediction of numeric variables. Path P3 in the figure shows the steps to predict aggregate data in the data warehouse environment. These steps involve generation of clusters, ranking of variables, STAR schema generation, data cube construction, building of classification models, evaluation of models, selection of a model and prediction of aggregate data.

Consider a real world mixed variables data set D of *Movies, Concerts and TV Shows* from *IMDB database* having four numerical and five nominal variables with 432 records in it. Numeric variables include *User Rating, No. of Votes, US Box Office Gross, and Cast (number)*. The nominal variables include *Title Type, Genres, Title Groups, Company, Production Status*. Nominal variables are given in the Table 1 along with their respective distinct values.

3.2 PATTERN EXTRACTION

This section presents the first part of the proposed framework called Pattern Extraction. As discussed above, this part works through a series of steps where each step takes input from the previous step. The steps involve hierarchical clusters generation, ranking of variables, multi-dimensional scaling, schema generation, mining of association rules, advanced evaluation of association rules and visualization of extracted patterns. The sub sections below explain each step briefly and then provide implementation using the example dataset.

3.2.1 Generate Hierarchical Clusters

In the first step of the model, *Agglomerative Hierarchical Clustering* is applied to all data based on numerical variables to generate clusters at different levels in the hierarchy. This step generates the dendrogram presenting each level by a set of child clusters linked to the single parent available at upper level. One issue related to hierarchical clustering is to determine at which point the generation of dendrogram is terminated. One way to find out the cut-off point

Table 1. Distinct Values for nominal variables in the example dataset D

Variables	Distinct Values
Title Type	Feature Film, TV Movie, TV Series, TV Episode, TV Special, Mini-Series, Documentary, Video Game, Short Film
Genres	Action, Adventure, Animation, Biography, Comedy, Crime, Documentary, Drama, Family, Fantasy, Film-Noir, Game-Show, History, Horror, Music, Musical, Mystery, News, Reality-TV, Romance, Sci-Fi, Sport, Talk-Show, Thriller, War, Western
Title Groups	Now-Playing, Oscar-Winning, Best Picture-Winning, Best Director-Winning, Oscar-Nominated, Emmy Award-Winning, Emmy Award-Nominated, Golden Globe-WinninG, Golden Globe-Nominated, Razzie-Winning, Razzie-Nominated, National Film Board Preserved
Company	20th Century Fox, Sony, DreamWorks, MGM, Paramount, Universal, Walt Disney, Warner Bros
Production Status	Released, Post-production, Filming, Pre-production, Completed, Script, Optioned Property, Announced, Treatment/outline, Pitch, Turnaround, Abandoned, Delayed, Indefinitely Delayed, Active, Unknown

is the use of linkage inconsistency threshold defined by authors in (Cordes, Haughton, Carew, Arfanakis, & Maravilla, 2002). The threshold is defined as:

$$lTh\left(link1\right) = \frac{lenght\left(link1\right) - \mu\left(all\,links\right)}{\sigma\left(all\,links\right)} \tag{1}$$

The links and heights used in the threshold calculation are shown in Figure 2. In order to calculate the mean length values across all links, height information is used with inconsistency coefficient. The length of link, link 1 represents the distance between two clusters. The μ variable indicates the mean of all links in the dendrogram, whereas σ is represented as the Standard Deviation across all links. The similarity of clusters linked by the link is inversely proportional to the threshold value. In other words, the threshold value determines the number of clusters without considering the domain knowledge. Within the cluster divisions, an abrupt change in similarity between data objects can be found by the inconsistency coefficient of links. If the height of a link is noticeably greater than the height of other link in the cluster below it, it indicates that there is no distinct division between clusters at that level in the hierarchy. The diagram shows that the links o top are inconsistent as compared to the links at the bottom of hierarchy.

The threshold is determined at such level in the hierarchy and taken as a cut-off point. Each cluster is given a label and we extract data at each level using Hierarchical clustering explorer. It is worth mentioning that the clustering is achieved more faithfully in AHC as compared to other existing approaches as cited by(Usman, Pears, & Fong, 2013). As in other approaches, AHC has full emphasis on numerical variables during clustering process. During clustering, nominal variables do not impact on the results, no mapping is required and original data of nominal variables is returned in the results. Euclidean distance measure is used to separate clusters at different levels in the hierarchical clustering process.

The illustrate the first step of model using the exemplary dataset D, AHC algorithm is applied on the numeric columns to generate clusters at different levels. It produces clusters which are numbered manually at each level and presented using a tree structure in Figure 4.

It is important to note that there are different variables involved in split of the clusters at each level. Moreover, each variable in every cluster will have a different variance than in the other cluster at same level. If all numeric

Figure 2. Dendrogram structure indicating links and associated heights

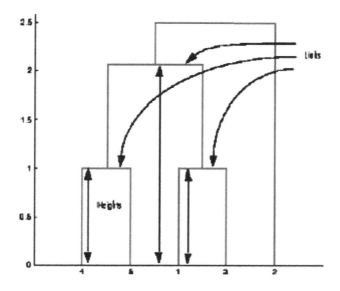

Figure 3. Dendrogram showing consistent and inconsistent links

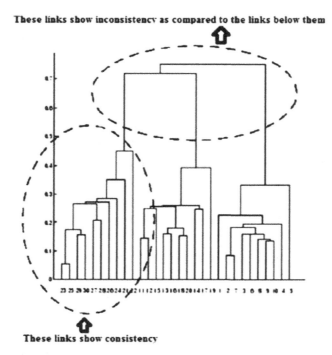

Figure 4. Tree structure of hierarchical clusters

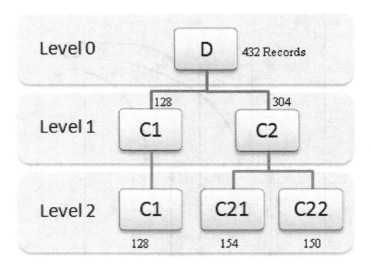

variables *User Rating, No. of Votes, US Box Office Gross, and Cast (number)* were used to define the split of C2 into C21 and C22, then a variable having an impact on split will have greater variance in one of the child clusters and lesser in the other cluster. At this stage all data in the example dataset is available in different clusters are different levels.

3.2.2 Rank Variables

After the dendrogram is created, the model applies Principal Component Analysis to rank the variables within each cluster. However since PCA only works on numeric data, the model applies another technique to convert nominal data into the numeric data to apply PCA. The model takes data of all nominal variables and converts it to numeric values using Rosarios's Approach(Rosario, Rundensteiner, Brown, Ward, & Huang, 2004).

3.2.2.1 Convert Nominal Variables to Numeric Variables

A review of Rosario's approach is now presented. Rosario's method uses Distance-Quantification-Classing approach. The distance step performs the transformation where as Quantification step assigns order and spacing among nominal values based on distance information. Rossario's approach addresses two problems mainly. First is to effectively assign distance and order among values. Second is to group similar values to reduce no. of distinct values. This process is multivariate, i.e it uses relationship of nominal variables to the other variables to decide ordering, spacing and classing of the values. It is also distance preserving, so distance between nominal variables is preserved after conversion. Similarly association is also preserved among variables after conversion.

In order to explain the Rosario's conversion approach, C2 cluster is taken to apply this methodology. Input files for the cluster are prepared for the tool used for this method and conversion is performed. The quantified versions of selected variables in a Parallel Coordinates display are shown in Figure 5.

In parallel coordinates, each vertical line represents one variable, and each polyline cutting across the vertical axes represents instances in the dataset. The nominal variables *Title Type, Genres, Title Groups, Company, Production Status* are shown using vertical lines, where as distinct values with order and spacing are shown on the vertical lines. The variables are ordered such that the vertical axes of highly associated variables are positioned next to each other for easier interpretation. The semantic relationship is clear between nominal variables through polylines in the diagram. Once the process is completed, all data of cluster C2 is available in numeric format.

Figure 5. Quantification display of Rossario's approach in parallel coordinates for cluster C2

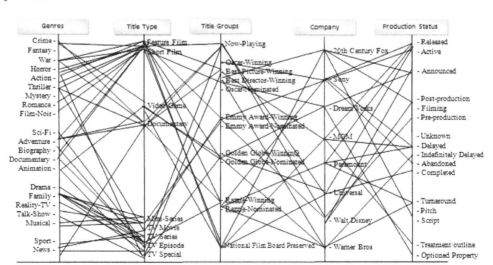

3.2.2.2 Apply Principal Component Analysis (PCA)

After the data is available in the numeric format, Principal Component Analysis is applied in order to measure the degree of variance for each variable and rank variables in the cluster. A review of PCA is now presented. Suppose that the data set under analysis contains n variables. PCA transforms the original set of variables to a small subset of variables which contain most variations. The variables with zero variance are ignored in the process. This is done by developing a set of Eigen Vectors (E_1, E_2 ,..., E_n). Suppose we have a data set A, we first project this data set to another data set A' having all numeric variables. A covariance matrix M is developed which represents the covariance of every item-pair. If Q is the diagonal matrix T of all possible Eigen vectors can be obtained using T-1MT= $^\Phi$. A set of factor loadings is developed from the set of Eigen Vectors from this expression. Only a subset of Eigen Vectors t% of the total variance across A' is used. Any Eigen vector can be presented by E_i and its association with a value e_i which contains the proportion of variance for that Eigen Vector. All vectors are ranked by their Eigen values. Once this is done, a subset is obtained by taking top m vectors which collectively capture at least t%, and are used for factor loading. The following equation represents the factor loading of a variable V:

$$F_i = \sum_{j=1}^{m} \left(E_{ij}\right)^2 - \forall i = 1,\ldots, \text{ n} \tag{2}$$

The ranking of numerical variables is produced using the factor loading F_i.

Since the model pretends to find ranking of variables in cluster C1, PCA is applied on its child clusters C21 and C22. Factor loading for numerical variables presented in these clusters is taken. The difference of factor loading of a numerical variable across child cluster is compared. Every variable at parent cluster is assigned a rank which is equal to the difference of factor loading of that variable in child clusters. The difference of factor loadings is directly proportional to the ranks. As difference increases, the higher rank is obtained for that variable. The ranking of variables is given in Table. 3.2.

In C2 cluster, it is clear that *Title Groups, Genres* and *Gross* are top ranked variables, and these variables have split this cluster from the data set. The model is able to pick top ranked variables for mining purposes in the later stages of the process.

3.2.3 Apply Multi-Dimensional Scaling

After the variables are ranked, the model defines natural grouping of all nominal variables involved in the prediction process. This process is called multi-dimensional scaling. A review of the grouping process is presented now. The multi-dimensional scaling allows grouping different distinct values of a variable together. Thus distinct values which are not far away from each other are placed in a single group. This grouping is based upon the algorithm defined by (Usman et al., 2013).The algorithm presented by the authors finds the minimum and maximum values in the variables, and also defines a threshold value. The algorithm starts by creating a group. It then puts first value in the group and moves forward. The algorithm takes next value and calculates the difference of that value from the last value in the group. If the difference is less than the threshold, it puts the value in the same group. In else case, a new group is created. By the end of the process, a list of groups is achieved where similar distinct values are put in same group and a Group-Others is also created which contains the values not included in any of the other groups.

By using the above technique, implementation of the scaling is presented now. The data is passed to the application developed by (Usman et al., 2013). The generated groups are saved for mining purposes in the next step. It is important to note that, similar distinct values are put in the same group as described above. For instance *Genre* variable may have different groups like Group1, Group2, etc. Group 1 for *Genres* can contain *Action, Adventure,*

Table 2. Ranking of variables in cluster C1

Rank	Variable	Type	C11 Factor Loading	C12 Factor Loading	Comparison Result
1	Title Groups	Nominal	0.854	0.419	0.435
2	Genres	Nominal	0.821	0.429	0.392
3	Gross	Numeric	0.711	0.350	0.361
4	Company	Nominal	0.762	0.452	0.310
5	User Rating	Numeric	0.777	0.486	0.291
5	Title Type	Nominal	0.921	0.665	0.256
7	No. of Votes	Numeric	0.881	0.667	0.214
8	Cast	Numeric	0.661	0.545	0.116
9	Status	Nominal	0.692	0.598	0.094

Crime, Horror, Mystery, Thriller, War. Another group of *Genres* can contain *Drama, Family, Music, Musical* values for example. At this stage, the process obtains a list of groups against top-ranked nominal variables for their distinct values for further processing. Groups of one variable are shown in Figure 7.

3.2.4 Generate Star Schema

After grouping has been obtained, the model takes nominal variables as dimensions and numeric variables as facts to create a multidimensional STAR schema. A review of STAR schema is now presented. STAR schema is the simplest form of a dimensional model where data is organized in facts and dimensions. A fact is generally an event that is counted or measured, for example sales, registrations etc. A dimension is defined as the reference to the fact, for example date, product or a student. A STAR schema can be visualized as the fact table in center surrounded by all dimension tables. Importantly, fact table contains all facts and referenced foreign keys to the dimension tables. Thus fact table contains aggregated information against different dimensions for different facts.

The implementation of STAR schema done in this research has two phases. In first phase, the STAR schema is generated where as the second phase involves movement of data in the schema structure. Both processes are automated. The STAR schema against a cluster is generated by using Algorithm 1. A review of Algorithm 1 is presented below.

Algorithm 1 takes Dataset, Numeric Columns, Nominal Columns and the Cluster as inputs and generates schema for the cluster which is an SQL Script. Steps 1-6 of the schema defines different variables to be used in the algorithm. Steps 7-8 create the fact table of the schema. Steps 9-13 of the algorithm create facts in the fact table by taking all numeric columns. The nominal variables are used to add each dimension as a foreign key in the steps 14-20. Steps 24-32 are used to create dimension tables and associate the foreign keys created in the previous steps to these tables. At the end a schema for the whole cluster is returned. This schema generates the fact table having all facts and all foreign keys for the dimensions, along with the dimension tables. It is worth mentioning here, that the dimension tables contain groups instead of distinct values along with another column containing list of distinct values in that group.

After the STAR schema is available, the second algorithm is used to move the data from cluster 2 to this schema. Algorithm 2 has been created to fully

Algorithm 1. Multidimensional schema generation

Input: Dataset // the name of dataset
              Numeric_Columns // list of numeric columns
              Nominal_Columns // list of nominal columns
              Cluster // cluster
Output: Schema // schema for data warehouse
Method: Generate Schema
              //initialize input variables
1:   *data_set* ← d
2:   *numeric_columns* ← $n_1, n_2, n_3, ..., n_i$
3:   *nominal_columns* ← $m_1, m_2, m_3, ..., m_k$
4:   *cluster* ← *c*
              //global schema variable
5:   *schema* ← ""
6:   *fact_table_schema* ← ""

              //create fact table
7:   *fact_table_name* ← "fact_" & *cluster*
8:   *fact_table_schema* ← table name is fact_table_name
              //add measures
9:   **foreach** *NumericColumn* c_i
10:     *col_name* ← *numeric_columns[i]*
11:     *fact_table_schema* ← add col_name to the schema
12: **endfor**
13: *f_keys* ← ""
              //add dimensions
14: **foreach** *NominalColumn* nc_j
15:     *col_name* ← *nominal_columns[j]* & "_id"
16:     *fact_table_schema* ← add *col_name* to the schema
17:     //name of dimension table to refer
18:     *dim_table* ← *cluster* & "_" & *nominal_columns[j]*
19:     *f_keys* ← add *col_name* as foreign_key
20: **endfor**

              //add foreign keys script
22: *fact_table_schema* ← *fact_table_schema* & *f_keys*
              //add the fact table schema to the output schema
23: *schema* ← *schema* & *fact_table_schema*
              //create dimension tables using nominal columns
24: **foreach** *NominalColumn* nc_k
25:     *p_key* ← *nominal_columns[k]* + '_id'
26:     *grp* ← *nominal_columns[k]* + '_group'
27:     *name* ← *nominal_columns[k]* + '_name'
              //create table for dimension
28:     *table_name* ← *cluster* & "_" & *nominal_columns[k]*
29:     *dim_table_schema* ← table name as table_name
30:     *dim_table_schema* ← add col list *p_key, grp, name*
              //add the *dim_table_schema* to the global script
31:     *schema* ← *schema* & *dim_table_schema*
32: **endfor**
33. **return** *schema*;

automate this movement of data. The data is moved and groups are chosen on the basis of distinct values of each variable in a particular instance.

This algorithm takes the dataset name, list of columns and fact table name as inputs and generates a script of SQL Queries, which can be used to import data into the schema. Steps 1-4 in the algorithm create variables to be used in the algorithm. Steps 5-19 generate queries for the import process. Against each row in the original data, it checks the type of each column. If the column type is numeric, the data is treated as fact. If the type is nominal, the foreign key is created by checking the respective dimension table. The process is run for each of the columns and at the end a query is created for this particular row. After the queries are created against all rows, the complete script is returned by the algorithm.

Algorithm 2. Import of data into the data warehouse

Input: *data_table* // the name of dataset
　　　fact_table // cluster
　　　columns // all columns for data table
Output: *Script* // script to import data in data warehouse
Method: Generate Script
//initialize input variables
1:　*columns* ← $n_1, n_2, n_3, ..., n_i$
2:　*data_table* ← *tbl*
3:　*fact_table* ← *fct_tbl*
　　//global script variable
4:　*import_script* ← ""

　　　//each row in original needs to be copied
5:　**foreach** *Row r_i*
　　　//for each row, prepare an insert statement
6:　　*fact_query* ← Insert Row query for *fct_tbl*
　　　//go through all columns
7:　　**foreach** *Column c_j*
　　　　//in case of nominal column
　　　　//separate entry in dimension table is done.
9:　　　**if**(type (c_j) == nominal)
　　　　　//insertion script for dimensional table
10:　　　*dim_query* ← script to create a row
　　　　　//take last inserted id and add it to
　　　　　//current row being moved to fact table
11:　　　*last_id* ← Run_Script(*dim_query*)
12:　　　　*dimension_tables_script* ← add *dim_query*
13:　　　　*fact_query* ←append c_j&"_id="& *last_id*
14:　　**else**
15:　　　*fact_query* ← append c_j & " = " $r_i[c_j]$
16:　　**endif**
17:　　**endfor**
18:　　*import_script* ← append *fact_query*
19:　**endfor**

20:　**return** *import_script*;

As discussed above, this step in the model has two phases. The first phase is based on Algorithm 1, which enables generation of the STAR schema. The second phase takes the STAR Schema and moves the data from original data set to this schema using Algorithm 2.

This whole process is now illustrated using the exemplary data set. The information of Dataset, Numeric Columns, Nominal Columns and Cluster is passed to the tool as shown in the Figure 6. The tool generates a schema which is saved in the SQL Queries format. After that, it's passed to SQL server to create the schema. The STAR schema generated by the process contains a fact table and three dimension tables. The top-ranked variables from previous step are used for this schema. The left side schema is generated using Algorithm 2. The schema is shown in Figure 7. The tool shown in Figure 6 generates the update statements on right side, and used to import the data. This part is done using Algorithm 2.

Since in the example dataset, cluster C2 was used to generate schema, a fact table with name IMDB_C2_Fact_Table is created. The top ranked dimensions were used to create three dimension tables: IMDB_C2_Genres, IMDB_C2_Company, and IMDB_C2_TitleGroup. The fact table contains all numeric columns as facts and all dimension names as foreign keys to the respective dimension tables. It is also important to note that the information of groups is helpful in order to define dimensional hierarchy. In every cluster, all dimensions have a group level and a value level. For example, if GENRES is taken as a dimension then it has GENRES (all) Level ' GENRES _GROUPS (GROUP) LEVEL ' GENRES _NAMES (VALUE) LEVEL.

3.2.5 Mine Association Rules

After the schema is generated and data is in the data warehouse, the model extracts patterns in the form of association rules. Association rule mining is a data mining technique to extract frequent item sets from a data set. Such rules can be defined by an implication link A→B where A and B are disjoint sub sets from the item set and are considered to be frequent in the data. Two thresholds are defined by the users called minimum confidence and minimum support. The rules generated using these thresholds are usually informative. The term support is defined for an item set as its proportion in the whole data set which contains this item set. The confidence of an item set A→B is defined as the percentage of records which have B provided that it also contains A. A generated rule is significant if it meets the given thresholds defined by the user. Generally association rule mining is applied on transaction databases.

Figure 6. View of prototype to used to generate multi-dimensional schema

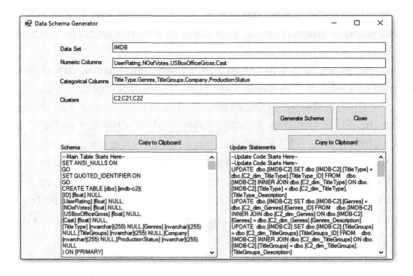

Figure 7. Multidimensional schema for cluster C1

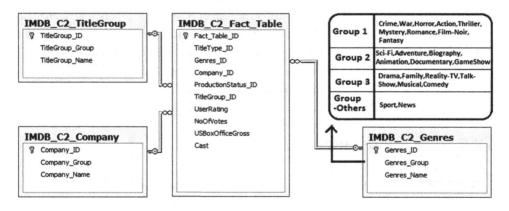

Such extraction helps to find the interesting relationship which might exist between different item sets within the database.

Suppose that I={ i_1 , i_2 ,..., i_n } is the set of n items. Each transaction T from this item set is obtained such that T ⊆ I. Moreover an association rule from same transactions can be defined as A→B such that A ⊆ B, B⊆ I, and A∩ B = $^\Phi$. The left side of any rule is called antecedent and the right side is called consequent. To understand the association rules in real world, if customer as bought butter, he will also buy bread, however the minimum thresholds for support and confidence will also be applicable. Support and confidence define the correlation between item sets in terms of significance and degree. We can conclude that in association rule mining, all rules are extracted which have greater support and confidence than the user defined thresholds.

Association rule mining is a two step process. In the first step frequent item sets are generated. In order to extract the frequent item sets, downward closure principle is used. Downward closure principle defines that any subset of a frequent item set is also frequent. This principle helps to prune the data more efficiently. The second step of association rule mining generates association rules from the frequent item sets from first step.

The implementation of association rule mining is now presented on the example data set. The cluster C2 is used as before, the schema and data generated in previous step is used in this stage. The model applies association rule mining on the schema in order to find the frequent patterns. Additionally, mining is also applied on original data as well in order to find if the schema results generates more informative rules than the rules generated from original data. In order to extract rules from multidimensional schema as well as the original data, the *Apriori* Algorithm is applied. In the rule mining step, the results of our ranking step are involved. Only highly ranked nominal variables are used as dimensions to identify the associations between them which will be significant as because of their high ranks.

Since PCA provides the degree of variation and their effectiveness on the whole item set, the highly ranked variables generate more informative rules. Some rules generated for cluster C1 are shown in Table 3 without the schema. The left hand side of the rules includes groups instead of distinct values of the variables, which allows getting patterns for group of values rather than distinct values. The rules with rules generated from same cluster using the schema are shown in Table 4 which significantly shows the difference between

Table 3. Rules for cluster C1 without multidimensional schema

Without Multidimensional Schema	
Rules	**Importance**
If TG* [Best Picture-Winning] →ProductionStatus [Released]	0.67
If Genres [Mystery] → Company [20th Century Fox]	0.58
If Company [Sony] & TG* [Best Director-Winning]→ Title Type [Feature Film]	0.54

*TG = Title Groups

Table 4. Rules for cluster C1 with multidimensional schema

With Multidimensional Schema	
Rules	Importance
If TitleGroups[Group2] → Company [20th Century Fox]	1.03
If Genres [Group1] & TitleGroups [Group3] → Company [Paramount]	1.01
If TitleGroups [Group1] & Genres [Group2]→ Company [Paramount]	0.73

importance values of top-generated rules. For instance, the top generated rule using the previous approach has an importance value of 0.67 where as the proposed model achieves 1.03 importance for the same cluster.

3.2.6 Evaluate Association Rules Using Advance Measures

Once the rules are obtained, these are evaluated using advanced measures. In order to measure the diversity criteria for interestingness, Rae, CON, Hill measures are applied as proposed by (Zbidi, Faiz, & Limam, 2006).These measures provide the evidence that the diversity of rules generated from our multidimensional schema is higher as compared to the diversity generated for rules without schema for same clusters. The diversity measures are applied to create a summary table. These tables are subsets of main data set according to a given rule. The interestingness is calculated using summary tables. Rae, CON, Hill are defined as below:

$$\text{Rae} = \sum_{i=0}^{m} \frac{ni\left(ni - 1\right)}{N\left(N - 1\right)} \tag{3}$$

$$\text{CON} = \sqrt{\frac{\left(\sum_{i=1}^{m} Pi^2\right) - \overline{q}}{1 - \overline{q}}} \tag{4}$$

$$\text{Hill} = 1 - \frac{1}{\sqrt{\sum_{i=1}^{m} Pi^3}} \tag{5}$$

Here, the number of rows in a summary table is defined as; n_i is the value of derived count of each row in the summary table. Total count is expressed by $N = \sum_{i=1}^{m} in$; $P_i = \dfrac{n_i}{N}$. The actual probability of row r_i; $\bar{q} = \dfrac{1}{m}$ is the uniform probability of row r_i.

The rules from previous step are taken to measure for interestingness. Rules are ranked using these measures in terms of diversity. This process has to be done at different levels of hierarchy in general (although current implementation is being described on a single cluster C2). Since it's a cumbersome process, this research includes development of a tool to generate diversity values dynamically for a cluster. The tool is shown in Figure 8. Table 5 describes the diversity values without multidimensional schema and with proposed model for generated rules for cluster C1. It is clear from Table 5 that the diversity values are better for multidimensional schema as compared to without schema values.

Figure 8. A view of diversity calculation application developed

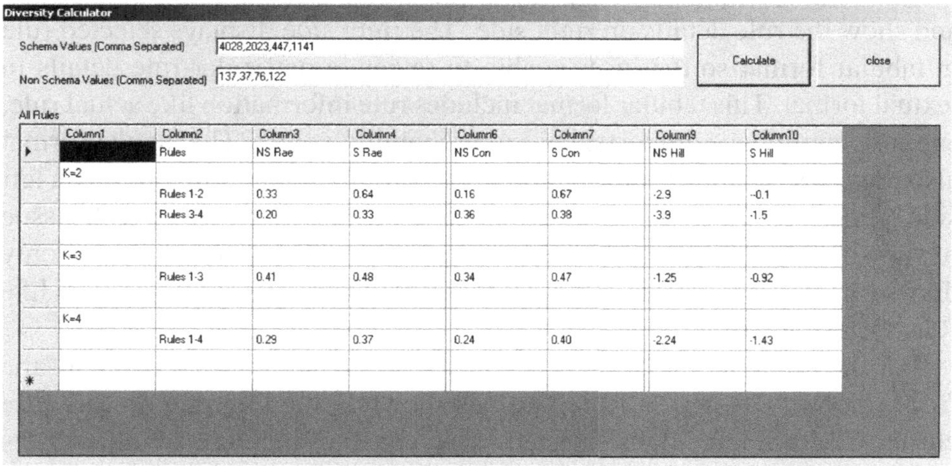

Table 5. Rules set Diversity without multidimensional schema

Without Multidimensional Schema			With Schema (% increase)		
Rule Set	**Rae**	**CON**	**Hill**	**Rae**	**CON**	**Hill**
R1-R2	0.33	0.36	-2.9	0.64 (**48%**)	0.67 (**46%**)	-0.1 (**28%**)
R3-R4	0.20	0.16	-3.9	0.33 (**39%**)	0.38 (**58%**)	-1.5 (**87%**)

3.2.7 Visualize Association Rules

The mining process discussed in the previous steps allows the mining of association rules from large datasets. The process is also assisted by a visualization component. The visualization component is broken into two parts, which allows the user to dig out the rules in a particular cluster, and a rule set with any size rather than whole data set at once. The first part is called "Clusters + Rule Sets". In this part, user is able to select a cluster in which rules are to be checked. Once a cluster is selected, rule sets in that cluster are shown on right side. The component has the ability to select a particular rule set size (K=2 up to K=10). The rule sets are shown using advanced measures like Rae, Con and Hill in a bubble chart format on x-y axis. Each bubble in the chart represents a rule set. The location of the bubble is defined by the average Rae and CON value on axis for each rule set. The size of the bubble represents the average importance of rules in a rule set. In third step, user selects a rule set to review this rule set which is passed to the second part of the visualization component. The second part "Association Rule Component" has two further parts. One part displays all rules graphically within the rule set selected in the previous step. It has the ability to select a rule on left side and show the rule details on right side. The right side displays selected rule in tabular format so that user is able to review a particular rule details in textual format. This tabular format includes rule information like actual rule, support, confidence, importance, and probability values. The tabular format also provides Grouping information of the variables which are placed on left side of the rule. Thus the visualization components smartly resolve the issue of showing large number of rules in a small space. The display also not only draws importance of rules, but plots the rules using advanced measures like Rae, CON and Hill.

For the example, the clusters of the dataset are shown on left side of the first window "Clusters + Rule Sets" as shown in the Figure 9. In this case cluster C2 from left side is selected, which enables the view of all rule sets of size K=2. As discussed before, K value can be up to 10. The right side shows the rule sets of size 2 in a bubble chart where the axis has Rae and Con values. The size of the bubble is determined by average importance of the rules in a particular rule set. By hovering the mouse on any bubble, rule set details can be reviewed which includes the advanced measures like Rae, Con, Hill and importance. Once a rule set is clicked, the process shifts to the second component called "Association Rules".

In the second window "Association Rules", the selected Rule Set is passed, and component displays all rules against that rule set as shown in Figure 10. If **K** has a value of 2, then two rules are displayed for the selected rule set. Similarly, if **K** has a value of 3 in the previous screen, a rule set of 3 rules is shown which was selected in previous window. Selection of any rule on left side shows the rule details on right hand side of this window. It is apparent that in this example, first rule is selected, which displays importance value on hover of mouse. The right hand side shows that particular rule. The rule information includes that actual rule, its support value, confidence value, importance value, probability of occurring, and grouping information. In this example the rule clicked has two grouping variables on left hand side, therefore two variables are shown at the bottom of the window along with their particular group's distinct values.

This component enhances the visual capability of the overall analysis. It is apparent that the issues discussed in literature review are resolved in the visualization component. The component resolves the issue of displaying lots of rules in a small space as well as accommodates advanced measures graphically.

3.3 PATTERN PREDICTION

This section presents the second module of the proposed framework called Pattern Prediction. As discussed above, this module works through a series of steps where each step takes input from the previous step. The process starts

Figure 9. Clusters and rule set information window of visualization component

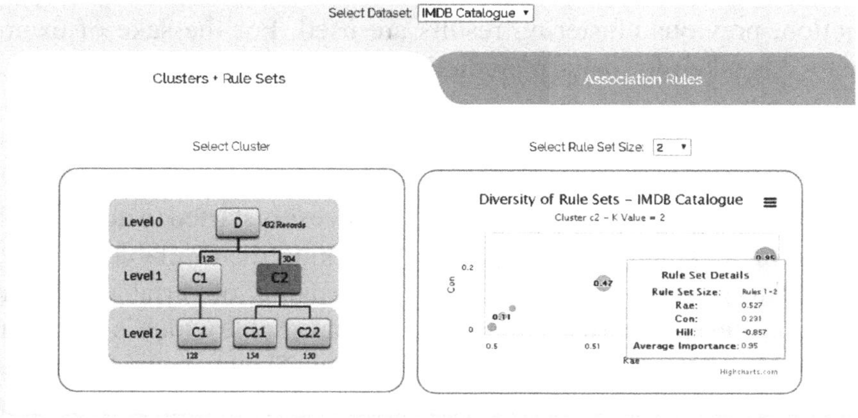

Figure 10. Association rules and their detailed information

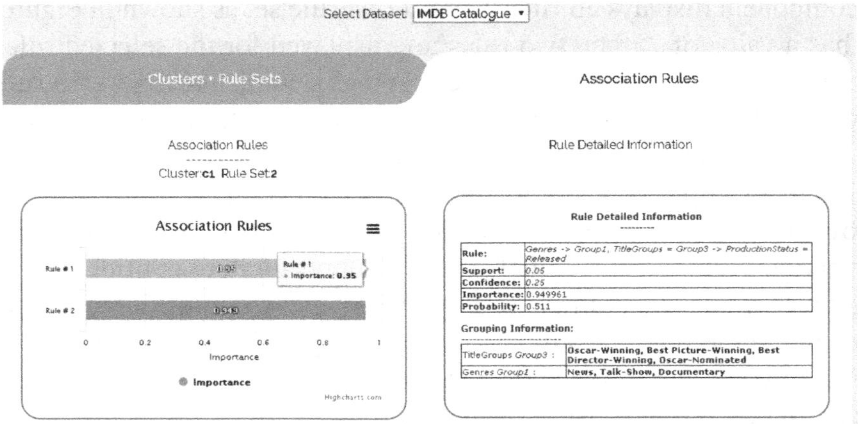

by obtaining hierarchical clusters and ranking of variables. After ranking, Path P1, P2 and P3 are adapted to derive a classification model, which is evaluated in the next step. The selection of path depends upon the nature of variable being predicted. After evaluation, a model is selected to predict the patterns. The sub sections below explain each step briefly and then provide implementation using the example dataset.

3.3.1 Generate Hierarchical Clusters

The first step in pattern prediction involves hierarchical clusters generation like pattern extraction. The step creates clusters at different levels in the hierarchy for further mining purposes. The hierarchical clustering mechanism has already been discussed in detail in pattern extraction section. For pattern prediction, previous clustering results are used. For the sake of example, cluster C2 is taken for pattern prediction in next step.

3.3.2 Rank Variables

Once the clusters are obtained, the ranking process is started to rank variables. In this component, a different process of ranking the available variables is adapted. This ranking process is based on normality of variables. A normal distribution presents the distribution of data in a variable which is symmetrical with a single central peak at mean of the data. The shape of the curve for normal distribution is described as bell-shaped. It is also termed at Guassian Curve. In a perfect normal distribution, fifty percent of the distribution lies to the left of mean and fifty percent lies to the right of the mean. The mean, median and mode are equal in a normal distribution. Figure 11 shows a perfect normal distribution curve.

For the example data set, the cluster C2 is used to draw normality results. Normality curves are drawn for each of the variable in the cluster and top ranked variables are picked. If a variable contains data which satisfies normality better than the other variables, it is considered to have more effect on classification. Figure 12 and Figure 13 present data of two variables.

It is easy to check the distribution of values within each variable. For example, in *Title Groups* variable, the distribution closely satisfies the bell-shaped curve. i.e all values are distributed normally with the middle value to the left and right. Whereas, *Production Status* has distribution of values in a

Figure 11. A perfect normal distribution with bell-shaped curve

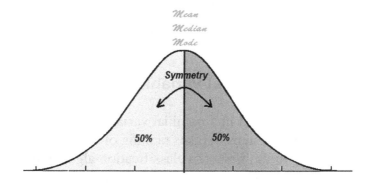

Figure 12. Normality Curve of Title Groups

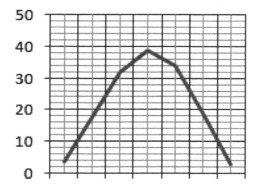

Figure 13. Normality Curve of Prod. Status

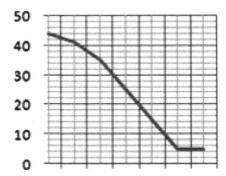

way that it cannot be picked out if compared with *Title Groups* variable. So *Title Groups* can be picked over *Production Status*. Ranking of all variables for cluster C2 is shown in Table 6. For prediction purposes, *Title Groups, Title Type and Genres* are ranked on top and can be used further.

Up to this point, the process has generated clusters, and one cluster has been picked. The ranking process has been applied and ranking of variables is available for prediction process. It now depends upon the variable types to be predicted. A review of three possibilities is now provided.

3.3.3 Prediction of Nominal Variable

If the variable to be predicted in a nominal variable the model adapts Path P1. This path is a series of steps. It takes ranking of variables as input along with the cluster data. In the first step classification algorithms are applied and results are gathered. These algorithms are evaluated using advanced measures in the next step to select a particular algorithm. In the last step actual prediction is done using the selected algorithm.

Table 6. Ranking of variables in cluster C2

Rank	Variable	Type	Rank	Variable	Type
1	Title Type	Nominal	6	Company	Nominal
2	Genres	Nominal	7	No. of Votes	Numeric
3	Gross	Numeric	8	Cast	Nominal
4	Title Groups	Nominal	9	Status	Numeric
5	User Rating	Numeric			

3.3.3.1 Apply Classification Algorithms

The model first generates association rules using Apriori Algorithm and calculates accuracy. The test is performed 10 times to get an average of accuracy. After that a set of classification algorithms is tested and results are calculated. The algorithms include Naïve Bayes, NN, VQNN, OWANN, J48, FuzzyNN, FONN and algorithms. A brief review of these algorithms is now presented.

Naive Bayes is a simple technique for constructing classifiers: models that assign class labels to problem instances, represented as vectors of feature values, where the class labels are drawn from some finite set. Naive Bayes classifiers assume that the value of a particular feature is independent of the value of any other feature, given the class variable. For example, a fruit may be considered to be an apple if it is red, round, and about 10 cm in diameter. A naive Bayes classifier considers each of these features to contribute independently to the probability that this fruit is an apple, regardless of any possible correlations between the color, roundness, and diameter features.

J48 is a predictive machine-learning model that decides the target value (dependent variable) of a new sample based on various attribute values of the available data. The internal nodes of a decision tree denote the different attributes, the branches between the nodes tell us the possible values that these attributes can have in the observed samples, while the terminal nodes tell us the final value (classification) of the dependent variable. The attribute that is to be predicted is known as the dependent variable, since its value depends upon, or is decided by, the values of all the other attributes. The other attributes, which help in predicting the value of the dependent variable, are known as the independent variables in the dataset. The J48 Decision tree classifier follows the following simple algorithm. In order to classify a new item, it first needs to create a decision tree based on the attribute values of the available training data. So, whenever it encounters a set of items (training set) it identifies the attribute that discriminates the various instances most clearly. This feature that is able to tell us most about the data instances so that we can classify them the best is said to have the highest information gain. Now, among the possible values of this feature, if there is any value for which there is no ambiguity, that is, for which the data instances falling within its category have the same value for the target variable, then we terminate that branch and assign to it the target value that we have obtained.

The nearest neighbour (NN) algorithm was one of the first algorithms used to determine a solution to the travelling salesman problem. In it, the salesman starts at a random city and repeatedly visits the nearest city until all have been visited. It quickly yields a short tour, but usually not the optimal one.

Below is the application of nearest neighbour algorithm to the travelling salesman problem. These are the steps of the algorithm:

1. Start on an arbitrary vertex as current vertex.
2. Find out the shortest edge connecting current vertex and an unvisited vertex
3. Set current vertex to V.
4. Mark V as visited.
5. If all the vertices in domain are visited, then terminate.
6. Go to step 2.

The sequence of the visited vertices is the output of the algorithm.

The theory of fuzzy sets is introduced into K-nearest neighbor technique to develop a fuzzy version of the algorithm. The fuzzy K-NN works well against other standard, more-sophisticated pattern recognition procedures.

VQNN (Vaguley Quantified Nearest Neighbor) is a variant of FRNN (Fuzzy Roughset nearest neighbor). VQNN handles noisy data very well. It has been proved that as the amount of noise in the data increases, VQNN performs increasingly better than FRNN, which shows that it is better in handling noisy data. VQNN performs statistically better than the other classification algorithms for increasing noise levels. OWANN, and FONN are also fuzzy variants of Nearest Neighbor algorithm.

For the cluster C2, model predicts *Company* by using top-ranked variables with the help of the above mentioned algorithms. For this purpose ARFF file is prepared for the WEKA tool. The tool inputs the file and produces classification results which are saved for further usage. For each algorithm 10-fold cross validation is used. The model calculates Accuracy, Recall, Precision and F-Measure for each algorithm and saves these. The results of these measures are passed to the next step for evaluation purposes.

3.3.3.2 Evaluate Using Advanced Measures

Once the results are ready, these results are passed to this step for advanced evaluation. This step allows the evaluation of algorithm based upon Accuracy, Recall, Precision and F-Measures. A review of these measures is now provided.

Accuracy is defined as the percentage of correctly classified instance by an algorithm during testing. Precision is the number of positive predictions divided by the total number of positive class values predicted. It is also called the Positive Predictive Value (PPV). Precision can be thought of as a measure of a classifier's exactness. A low precision can also indicate a large number of False Positives. Recall is the number of positive predictions divided by the number of positive class values in the test data. It is also called Sensitivity or the True Positive Rate. Recall can be thought of as a measure of a classifier's completeness. A low recall indicates many False Negatives. F-Measure is a measure of a test's accuracy. It considers both the precision p and the recall r of the test to compute the score. The score can be interpreted as a weighted average of the precision and recall, where an score reaches its best value at 1 and worst at 0. It is important to mention that since model works at 10 folds, it measures these values 10 times and takes the average of each measure for further usage.

This step also involves the visualization component which strengthens the process as well as enables the selection of an algorithm in better way. The visualization component allows the visualization of one algorithm at once. It involves a graphical display of Accuracy, Precision, Recall, and F-Measures along with the support to see the values in a tabular format. The table contains values for these measures along with the time taken in model building in milliseconds.

For the cluster C2, model predicts *Company* by using top-ranked variables with the help of the above mentioned algorithms. The results of the discussed measures above are given in the Table 7. From the results, it is evident that J48 and FONN perform better than all other algorithms. However, time taken by J48 algorithm is higher than FONN.

These results are further passed to the visualization component, which is shown in Figure 14. The left hand side of the visualization component shows advanced measures called Recall, Precision and F-Measure which makes it easier for the analyst to review. The middle section of the visualization component is shows the percentage of correctly and incorrectly classified instances based on the accuracy measure. These measures are further shown in tabular format on right side of the visualization component.

3.3.3.3 Predict Using Selected Algorithm

The last step of this process allows the selection of an algorithm from previous step and proceeds to prediction of the unknown instances based on the selected

Conceptual Model for Predictive Analysis on Large Data

Table 7. Evaluation results of classification algorithms

Algorithm	Accuracy	Time (ms)	Recall	Precision	F-Measure
NN	78.88 %	19	0.789	0.689	0.736
VQNN	78.88 %	26	0.789	0.689	0.736
OWANN	78.88 %	24	0.715	0.662	0.716
J 48	80.75%	124	0.807	0.743	0.769
FuzzyNN	77.92 %	21	0.790	0.901	0.801
FONN	80.75%	43	0.75	0.807	0.776
Naïve Bayes	79.50%	54	0.795	0.744	0.768
Apriori	45.89%	66	-	-	-

Figure 14. Visualization of advanced prediction measures

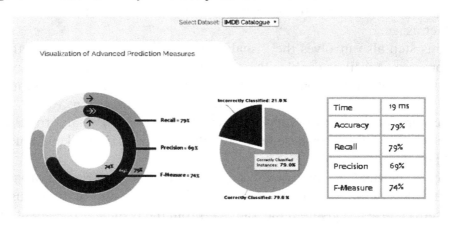

algorithm. The selection is based upon the values of advanced measures used in the model including Accuracy, Recall, Precision and F-Measure. The model also calculates Time for building the model which can also be considered for evaluation. For the example, the best suited algorithm is FONN which provides highest values for all measures and takes lesser time in model building than other algorithms.

3.3.4 Prediction of Numeric Variable

Likewise, if the variable to be predicted in a numeric variable the model adapts Path P2. This path is also a series of steps. It takes ranking of variables as input along with the cluster data from the previous stage like prediction of nominal variable. In the first step the process creates a STAR schema and then applies classification algorithms to gather results. These algorithms are evaluated using advanced measures in the next step like before to select a particular algorithm. In the last step actual prediction is done using the selected algorithm.

3.3.4.1 Generate STAR Schema

The input for this step is the cluster and top ranked variables. These variables are used to generate a STAR schema which is exploited further for prediction purposes. The schema generation process is same as described in the pattern extraction module. For the example dataset, the STAR schema is generated as shown in Figure 15. For example purposes, all dimensions are used in the schema as this schema will also be used for aggregate facts prediction in a data warehouse environment.

3.3.4.2 Apply Classification Algorithms

This step takes the STAR schema generated in the previous step as input and applies classification algorithms on it. The classification algorithms include Multi Layer Perceptron, Linear Regression and Simple Linear Regression since the predicted variable is numeric in this case. A review of these algorithms is now presented.

Figure 15. Multidimensional schema for cluster C1 to predict numeric variables

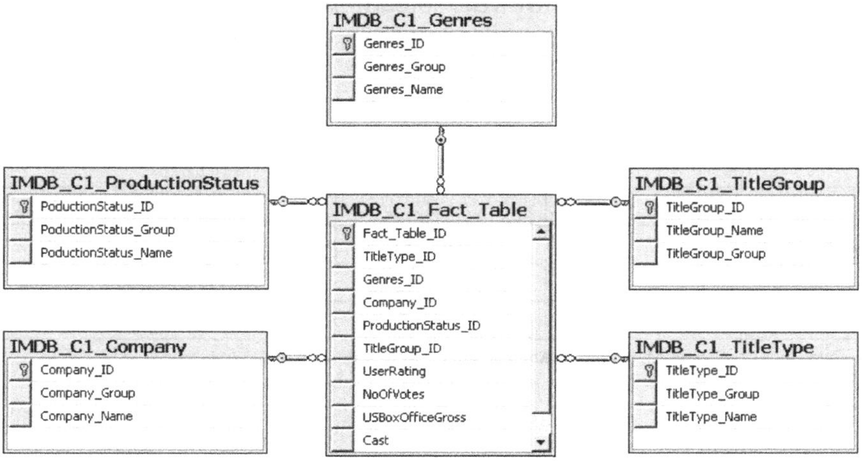

For the implementation of this step, the data is passed to WEKA tool like before and classification algorithms are applied. The variable *Normalized Losses* is predicted using the top-ranked variables. The evaluation measures are calculated for each of the algorithm for evaluation in the next step.

3.3.4.3 Evaluate Using Advanced Measures

After the classification algorithms are applied, the evaluation is done using measures namely Correlation Coefficient (CC), Mean absolute error (MSE), and Root mean squared error (RMSE). A review of these measures is now presented.

Correlation Coefficient (CC) is the measure defining the relationship between true value of interest and estimated value of the interest. Values closer to one predict the direct relationship, linear in general. RMSE is defined as Root Mean Squared Error which is used to measure the error rate of regression model. A lower value represents lower error rate. MAE is defined as Mean Absolute Error and has same unit as the original data. It is also an error rate similar to RMSE, but slightly lower in value. A lower value represents lower error rte.

For the example data, these measures are calculated against each algorithm in the previous step. The values retrieved through the process are shown in the Table 8. The table provides these measures against all algorithms used for the prediction of *US Box Office Gross*.

3.3.4.4 Predict Using Selected Algorithm

The last step of this process allows the selection of an algorithm from previous step and proceeds to prediction of the unknown instances based on the selected

Table 8. Evaluation of algorithms for prediction of US Box Office Gross

Algorithm	CC	MAE	RMSE
Multilayer Perceptron	0.9576	0.0308	0.2299
Simple Linear Regression	0.5429	0.3971	0.6519
Linear Regression	0.8741	0.1889	0.3764

CC = Correlation Coefficient, MAE = Mean Absolute Error, RMSE = Root Mean Squared Error

algorithm. The selection is based upon the values of advanced measures used in the model including Correlation Coefficient (CC), Mean absolute error (MSE), and Root mean squared error (RMSE). For the example, the best suited algorithm is Multilayer Perceptron. The Correlation Coefficient confirms that the prediction pattern is better and error rates MAE and RMSE are also lesser than the other models.

3.3.5 Prediction of Aggregate Data

The model also allows the prediction of aggregate data available in a multi-dimensional environment. In this case the model adapts Path P3. This path is also a series of steps. It takes ranking of variables as input along with the cluster data from the previous stage like prediction of aggregate data in the multi-dimensional environment. In the first step the process creates a STAR schema, generates data cube on top of the schema and then applies classification algorithms to gather results. These algorithms are evaluated using advanced measures in the next step like before to select a particular algorithm. In the last step actual prediction is done using the selected algorithm.

3.3.5.1 Generate STAR Schema

In this step, the process generates a STAR schema by using all variables. The numeric variables are taken as facts where as nominal variables are taken as dimensions. A dimension table is created against each of the nominal variables and a foreign key is created to link the fact table and dimension table. For the example purposes, the schema is generated for cluster C2 which is same as in the previous section.

3.3.5.2 Compute Data Cube

Once the STAR schema is ready, the model computes a data cube on the schema by importing all data from the cluster to this schema. The resultant data cube contains data in aggregate form. For example purposes, data of cluster C2 is imported in the data warehouse. Some sample data from the data cube is showing in Table 9. The numeric columns present the data in Average aggregate measure.

Table 9. Five records sample taken from data cube constructed on the schema

Title Type	Title Group	Genres	Company	Status	Rating	Votes	Gross	Cast
Feature Film	NW*	Action	Sony	Released	5.0	4542	8.0	12
Feature Film	OW**	Horror	MGM	Released	9.0	1341	18.0	45
TV Special	NW*	Action	Sony	Released	6.6	6752	12.0	27
TV Series	BPW***	History	Sony	Released	8.9	2472	11.0	32
Feature Film	OW**	Romance	MGM	Released	9.6	1733	33.0	65

* NW = Now Playing, ** OW = Oscar Winning, *** BPW = Best Picture Winning

3.3.5.3 Apply Classification Algorithms

This step takes the data cube generated in the previous step as input and applies classification algorithms on it. The classification algorithms include Multi Layer Perceptron, Linear Regression and Simple Linear Regression.

For the implementation of this step, the data cube generated in the previous step is taken as example and classification algorithms are applied. These algorithms predict Average *US Box Office Gross* with the help of *Title Group, Genres* and *Average No. of Votes*. The evaluation measures are calculated for each of the algorithm for evaluation in the next step.

3.3.5.4 Evaluate Using Advanced Measures

After the classification algorithms are applied, the evaluation is done using measures namely Correlation Coefficient (CC), Mean absolute error (MSE), and Root mean squared error (RMSE). For the example data, these measures are calculated against each algorithm in the previous step. The values retrieved through the process are shown in the Table 10. The table provides these measures against all algorithms used for the prediction of *US Box Office Gross* using the variables *Title Group, Genres and Average No. of Votes*.

Table 10. Evaluation Results of Classification Algorithms

Algorithms	CC	MAE	RMSE
Multilayer Perceptron	0.8434	0.0108	0.1100
Simple Linear Regression	0.6546	0.3072	0.5328
Linear Regression	0.7562	0.0329	0.2892

CC = Correlation Coefficient, MAE = Mean Absolute Error, RMSE = Root Mean Squared Error

3.3.5.5 Predict Using Selected Algorithm

The last step of this process allows the selection of an algorithm from previous step and proceeds to prediction of the unknown instances based on the selected algorithm. The selection is based upon the values of advanced measures used in the model including Correlation Coefficient (CC), Mean absolute error (MSE), and Root mean squared error (RMSE). For the example, the best suited algorithm is Multilayer Perceptron. The Correlation Coefficient confirms that the prediction pattern is better and error rates MAE and RMSE are also lesser than the other models.

3.4 SUMMARY

In this chapter, the proposed model has been explained with the help of an example data set. The pattern extraction module has been explained by taking a cluster on second layer, and by extracting associations rules from it with the methodology discussed above in detail. This component now only allows the extraction but doesn't involve the user in the process, allows automatic generation of schema at different levels, uses advanced measures of evaluation and provides a mean for the users to visualize the results. The pattern prediction component provides ability to select classification model that fits the data, with the help of a series of steps explained above. This component has the ability to apply multiple algorithms at once, and evaluate these based on advanced measures. The evaluation process also includes a visualization component to assist the user to select a particular algorithm for prediction purposes.

REFERENCES

Cordes, D., Haughton, V., Carew, J. D., Arfanakis, K., & Maravilla, K. (2002). Hierarchical clustering to measure connectivity in fMRI resting-state data. *Magnetic Resonance Imaging*, *20*(4), 305–317. doi:10.1016/S0730-725X(02)00503-9 PMID:12165349

Rosario, G. E., Rundensteiner, E. A., Brown, D. C., Ward, M. O., & Huang, S. (2004). Mapping nominal values to numbers for effective visualization. *Information Visualization*, *3*(2), 80–95. doi:10.1057/palgrave.ivs.9500072

Usman, M., Pears, R., & Fong, A. C. M. (2013). Discovering diverse association rules from multidimensional schema. *Expert Systems with Applications*, *40*(15), 5975–5996. doi:10.1016/j.eswa.2013.05.031

Zbidi, N., Faiz, S., & Limam, M. (2006). On mining summaries by objective measures of interestingness. *Machine Learning*, *62*(3), 175–198. doi:10.1007/s10994-005-5066-8

Chapter 4
Experimental Study I:
Automobile Dataset

ABSTRACT

This chapter provides implementation of the proposed model on Automobile data set. The chapter includes the implementation of pattern extraction from this dataset by following a series of steps discussed in the proposed model chapter. It also includes detailed implementation of pattern prediction from Automobile dataset for prediction of numeric variables, nominal variables, and aggregate data. The implementation of pattern prediction is also a series of steps as discussed before.

4.1 DATASET INTRODUCTION

This case study involves implementation of model using *Automobile* dataset which is available at UCI machine learning repository(Asuncion & Newman, 2007). This dataset is a mixture of numeric and nominal variables and contains 26 variables. There are 11 nominal (categorical) variables and 15 numeric variables. Nominal variables, along with their respective distinct values are given in Table 1. Numeric variables include *Wheel Base, Length, Width, Height, Curb Weight, Engine Type, Engine Size, Bore, Stroke, Compression Ratio, Horse Power, Peak RPM, City MPG, Highway MPG* and *Price*. This standard dataset describes the characteristics of an automobile. More details of the dataset are available at UCI machine learning website.

DOI: 10.4018/978-1-5225-5029-7.ch004

4.1.1 Generate Hierarchical Clusters

In the first step of the model, *Agglomerative Hierarchical Clustering* is applied to all data based on numerical variables to generate clusters at different levels in the hierarchy. A detailed discussion of this step has already been provided in the proposed model chapter. This step produces clusters which are numbered manually at each level and presented using a tree structure in Figure 1.

It is important to note that there are different variables involved in split of the clusters at each level. Moreover, each variable in every cluster will

Table 1. Nominal variables along with their distinct values from Automobile Dataset

Nominal Variables	Distinct Values
Make	alfa-romero, audi, bmw, chevrolet, dodge, honda, isuzu, jaguar, mazda, mercedes-benz, mercury, mitsubishi, nissan, peugot, plymouth, porsche, renault, saab, subaru, toyota, volkswagen, volvo
Fuel Type	diesel, gas
Aspiration	std, turbo
Number of doors	four, two
Body Style	hardtop, wagon, sedan, hatchback, convertible
Drive Wheels	4wd, fwd, rwd
Engine Location	front, rear
Engine Type	dohc, dohcv, l, ohc, ohcf, ohcv, rotor
No. of Cylinders	eight, five, four, six, three, twelve, two
Fuel System	1bbl, 2bbl, 4bbl, idi, mfi, mpfi, spdi, spfi
Symboling	-3, -2, -1, 0, 1, 2, 3

Figure 1. Tree structure of hierarchical clusters

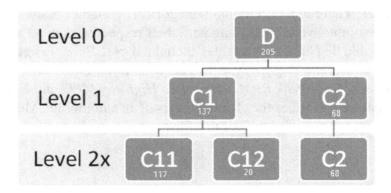

have a different variance than in the other cluster at same level. If all numeric variables *Wheel Base, Length, Width, Height, Curb Weight, Engine Type, Engine Size, Bore, Stroke, Compression Ratio, Horse Power, Peak RPM, City MPG, Highway MPG* and *Price* were used to define the split of C1 into C11 and C12, then a variable having an impact on split will have greater variance in one of the child clusters and lesser in the other cluster. At this stage all data in the example dataset is available in different clusters are different levels.

4.1.2 Rank Variables

After the dendrogram is created, the model applies Principal Component Analysis to rank the variables within each cluster. However since PCA only works on numeric data, the model applies another technique to convert nominal data into the numeric data to apply PCA. The model takes data of all nominal variables and converts it to numeric values using Rosarios's Approach (Rosario, Rundensteiner, Brown, Ward, & Huang, 2004). A detailed discussion on this approach has already been provided in the proposed model chapter.

4.1.2.1 Convert Nominal Variables to Numeric Variables

To convert nominal variables to numeric variables, input files for the cluster are prepared for the tool used for this method and conversion is performed. The quantified versions of selected variables in a Parallel Coordinates display are shown in Figure 2 for cluster C11.

Figure 2. Quantification display of Rossario's approach in parallel coordinates for cluster C11

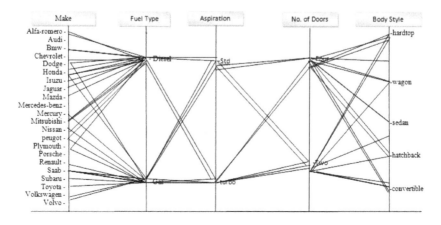

Since the dataset contains 11 nominal columns, due to lack of space, only 5 columns are shown in the parallel coordinates in the diagram. In parallel coordinates, each vertical line represents one variable, and each polyline cutting across the vertical axes represents instances in the dataset. The nominal variables *Make, Fuel Type, Aspiration, No. of Doors, Body Style* are shown using vertical lines, where as distinct values with order and spacing are shown on the vertical lines. The variables are ordered such that the vertical axes of highly associated variables are positioned next to each other for easier interpretation. The semantic relationship is clear between nominal variables through polylines in the diagram. Once the process is completed, all data of the clusters is available in numeric format.

4.1.2.2 Apply Principal Component Analysis (PCA)

After the data is available in the numeric format, Principal Component Analysis is applied in order to measure the degree of variance for each variable and rank variables in the clusters. A detailed discussion on PCA has already been provided in proposed model chapter. Figure 3 shows the ranking of numeric variables in the three clusters after performing the PCA. From the Figure 3, it is evident that the same variables have different ranks within the different clusters. In other words, every cluster contains a distinctive set of numeric variables on top of the list. For example, *Curb Weight*, *Width* and *Length* are top ranked variables in cluster C1.

Figure 3. Ranking of numeric variables using PCA for clusters C1, C11 and C12

C1		
Variable Name	Calculated Value	Rank
CURBWEIGHT	0.95	1
WIDTH	0.87	2
LENGTH	0.84	3
SYMBOLING	-0.16	14
PEAKRPM	-0.20	15
CITYMPG	0.20	16

C11		
Variable Name	Calculated Value	Rank
CURBWEIGHT	0.83	1
PRICE	0.78	2
HORSEPOWER	0.73	3
DRIVEWHEELS	-0.46	15
HIGHWAYMPG	-0.87	16
CITYMPG	-0.90	17

C12		
Variable Name	Calculated Value	Rank
COMPRESSIONRATIO	0.98	1
CITYMPG	0.98	2
HIGHWAYMPG	0.98	3
HORSEPOWER	-0.86	14
PRICE	-0.87	15
ENGINESIZE	-0.88	16

However, in the lower data abstraction level, for example, in C11, *Curb Weight* maintains its position, but *Width* and *Height* don't maintain their rank. In case of C11, the top ranked variables include *Price* and *Horse Power*. The situation is more interesting in case of C12, where none of the top 3 ranked variables in C1 appear on top and instead go well at the bottom of the list. The variable *Curb Weight* remained on top in C1 and C11, but was positioned 13th in C12. *Width* was ranked at 2nd position in C1 and it was ranked 4th in C11 whereas it went to 11th position in C12. *Length* variable was ranked at 3rd position in C1, and maintained its position in C11 as well, but it was ranked at 9th position in C12. We can conclude the cluster C1 is split into two clusters on the basis of Price and Horse Power mainly and on *Compression Ratio* marginally. Figure 4 shows the ranking of nominal variables in the three clusters after performing PCA.

In case of nominal variables, there is also a difference in ranking of variables at different levels. It can be seen from Figure 4 that top ranked variables, *Engine Type*, *Body Style* and *Engine Location* in C1 don't have same ranks in C11 and C12. The variable *Engine Type* is ranked at first position in C1. But this variable is ranked as 5th in C11. Same variable is ranked at 4th position in C12. *Body Style* was ranked at 2nd position in C1, and was found at 6th position in C12. Due to zero variance in C11, *Body Style* was not ranked at all. *Engine Location* was ranked at position 3 in C1. It was moved to 4th position in C11. Due to zero variance in C12, the variable was not ranked. The top ranked variable in C11 is *Make*, and it was ranked at 6th position in C1. The top ranked variable *Fuel Type* in C12 is ranked at 4th position in C1. It can be concluded that C1 cluster is split into two clusters on the basis of *Make*, *Fuel Type* and *Aspiration*.

4.1.3 Apply Multi-Dimensional Scaling

After the variables are ranked, the model defines natural grouping of all nominal variables involved in the prediction process. This process is called multi-dimensional scaling. A review of the grouping process is already provided in detail in previous chapter. The top ranked dimensions of C11 cluster are *Engine Type, Engine Style* and *Engine Location*. The *Engine Type* variable values are put into two groups. First group of *Engine Type* variable contains *rotor, dohc, ohcv, l* and *ohc*. The second group contains ohcf. It is clear from the group information that *Engine Type* values are naturally grouped together. Similarly other dimensions such as *Engine Size, Engine Location* etc also

Figure 4. Ranking of nominal variables using PCA for clusters C1, C11 and C12

C1		
Variable Name	**Calculated Value**	**Rank**
ENGINETYPE	0.95	1
BODYSTYLE	0.87	2
ENGINELOCATION	0.84	3
FUELTYPE	0.84	4
ASPIRATION	0.84	5
MAKE	0.73	6
FUELSYSTEM	0.60	7
NUMOFCYLINDERS	0.46	8
NUMOFDOORS	0.27	9

C11		
Variable Name	**Calculated Value**	**Rank**
MAKE	0.83	1
ASPIRATION	0.78	2
NUMOFCYLINDERS	0.73	3
ENGINELOCATION	0.68	4
ENGINETYPE	0.67	5
FUELSYSTEM	0.55	6
NUMOFDOORS	0.54	7

C12		
Variable Name	**Calculated Value**	**Rank**
FUELTYPE	0.95	1
ASPIRATION	0.98	2
FUELSYSTEM	0.98	3
ENGINETYPE	0.62	4
MAKE	0.21	5
BODYSTYLE	0.07	6

contain groupings which enlighten the semantic relationship present in these variables. Groups of one variable are shown in the Figure 5.

4.1.4 Generate STAR Schema

After grouping has been obtained, the model takes nominal variables as dimensions and numeric variables as facts to create a multidimensional STAR schema. A review of STAR schema has been given in previous chapters. This schema generation process is based on algorithms 1,2 as discussed in previous chapter. The resultant multidimensional schema for cluster C11 is show in Figure 5. The schema contains a fact table with name c11_Fact_Table. The top ranked dimensions were used to create three dimension tables: c11_noofcylinders, c11_make and c11_aspiration The fact table contains all numeric columns as facts and all dimension names as foreign keys to the respective dimension tables.

4.1.5 Mine Association Rules

After the schema is generated and data is in the data warehouse, the model extracts patterns in the form of association rules. A detailed discussion on association rule mining has already been provided in the previous chapter. Association rule mining is applied on top ranked variables to generate rules for a cluster, for example C11. The rules generated through this process have minimum .8 probability value and minimum importance value of 0.99.

Figure 5. Multidimensional schema for cluster C11

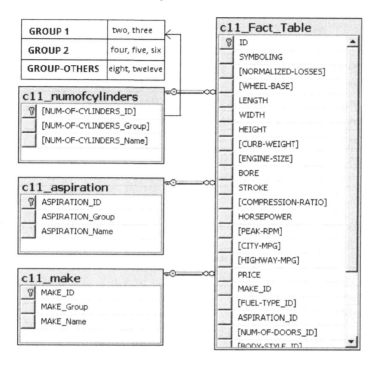

For cluster C11, the technique generates 8 rules. From the rules produced, it is clear that the low ranked variables have tendency to predict the *Make* of an automobile. The results show that the eight cylinder automobiles are only *Mercedes-Benz*. Similarly the *Number of Cylinders* and *Aspiration* can predict other *Make* when combined together. The effectiveness of this pattern extraction procedure is clear as it provides an abstract review of whole data set at once. In (Usman, Pears, & Fong, 2013), authors also provided a similar approach to mine patterns at multiple levels. A comparison of proposed approach with the previous approach is now presented.

Table 2 provides the list of rules generated for cluster C11 with the proposed technique and Table 3 shows the rules generated with the previous similar approach by (Usman et al., 2013). The top rule generated from proposed technique provides an importance of 1.9 as compared to the top rule of the set against which comparison is being made, which has 0.49 importance value for the same cluster. This means that the rules generated by proposed technique are more important than the other technique. Moreover, proposed technique generated all rules having importance value greater than or equal

Table 2. Rule generated from our proposed methodology

Rules	Imp.
1. No.of Cylinders Group=*Group1*,Aspiration Group=*Group-Others*→Make = *mercedes-benz*	1.90
2. No. of Cylinders Group = *Group 1* → Make = *mercedes-benz*	1.90
3. Aspiration Group = *Group 1* → Make = *audi*	1.64
4. No. of Cylinders Group = *Group 1*, Aspiration Group = *Group-Others* → Make =*audi*	1.31
5. No. of Cylinders Group = *Group 1*, Aspiration Group = *Group-Others* → Make =*audi*	1.17
6. No. of Cylinders Group = *Group 1* → Make = *mazda*	1.14
7. No. of Cylinders Group =*Group 1*, Aspiration Group = *Group-Others*→ Make = *mazda*	1.14
8. No. of Cylinders Group =*Group-Others*, Aspiration Group=*Group-Others*→Make = *nissan*	0.99

Table 3. Rules generated from the methodology proposed by (Usman et al., 2013)

Rules	Imp.
1. Body Style = *hatchback*, Drive Wheels = *rwd* → Doors = *two*	0.49
2. Body Style = *convertible* → Doors = *two*	0.36
3. Body Style = *convertible*, Drive Wheels = *rwd* → Doors = *two*	0.36
4. Body Style = *hardtop*, Drive Wheels = *rwd* → Doors = *two*	0.36
5. Body Style = *hardtop* → Doors = *two*	0.36
6. Body Style = *wagon* → Doors = *four*	0.26
7. Drive Wheels = *4wd*, Body Style = *hatchback* → Doors = *two*	0.22
8. Body Style = *wagon*, Drive Wheels = *fwd* → Doors = *four*	0.21
9. Body Style = *wagon*, Drive Wheels = *rwd* → Doors = *four*	0.18
10. Drive Wheels = *4wd*, Body Style = *wagon* → Doors = *four*	0.16

to 0.9. Whereas the other technique generates rules set in which top rule has 0.49 importance value. The same can be inferred from the comparison chart of rules of both techniques as in Figure 6.

It is evident from Figure 6, that proposed technique generates more important rules than the technique provided by (Usman et al., 2013). The most important rule generated from the technique in (Usman et al., 2013) has a value 0.49 where as the lowest important rule in our approach has a greater value of 0.99. It clearly indicates that proposed approach out performs the other technique.

Figure 6. Comparison chart of rules importance generated from our approach and (Usman et al., 2013) approach for cluster C11

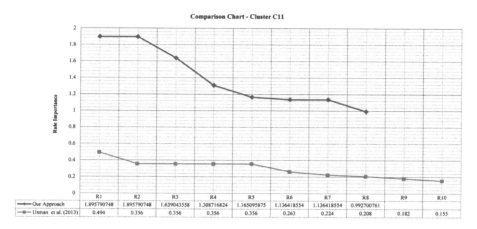

	R1	R2	R3	R4	R5	R6	R7	R8	R9	R10
Our Approach	1.895790748	1.895790748	1.639043558	1.308716824	1.165095875	1.136418554	1.136418554	0.992700761		
Usman et al. (2013)	0.494	0.356	0.356	0.356	0.356	0.263	0.224	0.208	0.182	0.155

4.1.6 Evaluate Association Rules Using Advance Measures

Once the rules are obtained, these are evaluated using advanced measures. As described in the example data set in previous chapter that extracted patterns must be validated with advanced measures in order to measure the interestingness for the user, diversity measures called Rae, CON, and Hill measures are applied on extracted patterns. The results are given in Table 4. The non-schema results are calculated as well in order to see the effectiveness of proposed approach.

It is evident that in most of the cases, the diversity values are better. However, since the data in this dataset has less number of records, therefore the diversity increase is not consistent.

4.1.7 Visualize Association Rules

The mining process discussed in the previous steps allows the mining of association rules from large datasets. The process is also assisted by a visualization component. The generated rules are visualized using a graphical interface in order to assist the analysts in the mining process. The interface contains two components. The first one is called "Clusters + Rule Sets". In Figure 7, the C11 cluster has been visualized in first component. The left side shows the clusters in the dataset, we choose C11 cluster to visualize. On

Table 4. Diversity results of cluster C11 by using the proposed model

Rule Sets		Rae		Con		Hill	
		Non Schema	Schema	Non Schema	Schema	Non Schema	Schema
K=2	Rules 1-2	0.60	0.50	0.60	0.10	-0.39	-0.97
	Rules 3-4	0.60	**0.68**	0.60	**0.62**	-0.39	**-0.36**
	Rules 5-6	0.33	**0.47**	0.33	0.17	-0.73	-0.92
	Rules 7-8	0.47	0.47	0.17	**0.33**	-0.92	**-0.73**
K=3	Rules 1-3	0.33	**0.48**	0.33	**0.47**	-1.38	**-1.05**
	Rules 4-6	0.17	**0.41**	0.25	**0.38**	-1.53	**-1.13**
K=4	Rules 1-4	0.27	**0.40**	0.35	**0.45**	-1.77	**-1.37**
	Rules 5-8	0.30	0.25	0.37	0.23	-1.66	-2.29
K=5	Rules 1-5	0.20	**0.38**	0.28	**0.48**	-2.54	**-1.47**
K=6	Rules 1-6	0.17	**0.35**	0.28	**0.48**	-2.98	**-1.61**
K=7	Rules 1-7	0.18	**0.34**	0.30	**0.48**	-3.07	**-1.69**
K=8	Rules 1-8	0.15	**0.33**	0.25	**0.49**	-4.07	**-1.74**

Figure 7. Visualization of pattern extraction process of cluster C11 (Component 1)

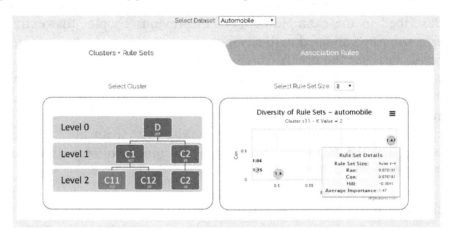

right side, the tool displays the rules sets based upon the size selected. The interface shows rule sets based on Rae and Con values on x and y axis. The average *importance* of a particular rule set decides the size of the bubble in the chart. Detailed information is provided on hover of a particular rule set including all advanced measures like Rae, Con, Hill and Importance.

After a specific rule set is selected to be explored further for rules inside, the user is shown the second tab called "Association Rules". This tab is shown in Figure 8. The left side of this tab shows all rules in the rule set. If the selected rule set had size 8, this tab will show 8 rules in that rule set. User is able to select any rule on left side to view more detailed information of the rule including the actual rule, its support, confidence, importance and probability on right side. The interface also allows user to review the grouping information of the variables involved on left side. We review the Rule # 2 in our case, which shows detailed information on right side. This information includes the rule details along with values of importance, support and confidence. Since the left hand side of the selected rule contains only a single variable, i.e *No. of Cylinders*, the grouping information against that variable is shown at the bottom. User can review any rule set like this along with its details.

4.2 PATTERN PREDICTION

This section presents the second module of the proposed framework called Pattern Prediction. As discussed in previous chapter, this module works through a series of steps where each step takes input from the previous step. The process starts by obtaining hierarchical clusters and ranking of variables. After ranking, Path P1, P2 and P3 are adapted to derive a classification model,

Figure 8. Visualization of pattern extraction process of cluster C11 (Component 2)

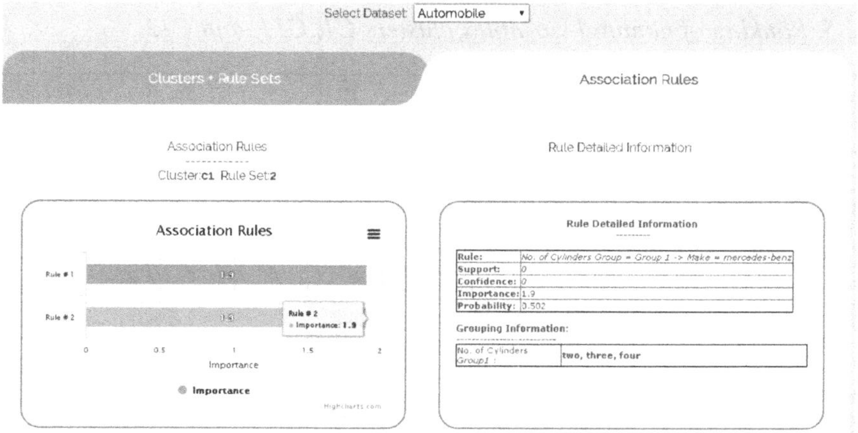

which is evaluated in the next step. The selection of path depends upon the nature of variable being predicted. After evaluation, a model is selected to predict the patterns. The sub sections below explain each step briefly and then provide implementation using the example dataset.

4.2.1 Generate Hierarchical Clusters

The first step in pattern prediction involves hierarchical clusters generation like pattern extraction. The step creates clusters at different levels in the hierarchy for further mining purposes. The hierarchical clustering mechanism has already been discussed in detail in pattern extraction section of previous chapter. For pattern prediction, previous clustering results are used. For the sake of example, cluster C2 is taken for pattern prediction in next step.

4.2.2 Rank Variables

Once the clusters are obtained, the ranking process is started to rank variables. In this component, a different process of ranking the available variables is adapted. This ranking process is based on normality of variables as discussed previously. Normality curves are drawn for each of the variable in each cluster and top ranked variables are picked. If a variable contains data which satisfies normality better than the other variables, it is considered to have more effect on classification. Ranking of numeric and nominal variables is given in Table 5 and 6 respectively.

Table 5. Ranking of nominal variables clusters C1, C11, and C12

Rank	C1	C11	C12
1	Engine Style	Engine Style	Make
2	Fuel Type	Make	Engine Style
3	Body Style	Body Style	Body Style
4	Make	Aspiration	Engine Location
5	Engine Location	Fuel Type	Fuel Type
6	Aspiration	Engine Location	No. of Doors
7	No. of Cylinders	Fuel System	No. of Cylinders
8	Fuel System	No. of Cylinders	Aspiration
9	No. of Doors	No. of Doors	Fuel System

Table 6. Ranking of Numeric variables clusters C1, C11, and C12

Rank	C1	C11	C12
1	City MPG	Width	Normalized Losses
2	Highway-MPG	Height	Peak-RPM
3	Height	City MPG	Height
4	Width	Length	City MPG
5	Stroke	Stroke	Width
6	Peak-RPM	Normalized Losses	Highway-MPG
7	Wheel Base	Wheel Base	Wheel Base
8	Normalized Losses	Highway-MPG	Stroke
9	Symboling	Symboling	Symboling
10	Length	Peak-RPM	Length

In our example, we find that, in C1, *Engine Style, Body Style and Engine Location* are ranked on top and thus can be used for prediction in this particular cluster. Similarly variables in each cluster are ranked separately. As discussed in proposed model in detail that the ranking process in this case is done using Normality.

4.2.3 Prediction of Nominal Variable

If the variable to be predicted in a nominal variable the model adapts Path P1. This path is a series of steps. It takes ranking of variables as input along with the cluster data. In the first step classification algorithms are applied and results are gathered. These algorithms are evaluated using advanced measures in the next step to select a particular algorithm. In the last step actual prediction is done using the selected algorithm.

4.2.3.1 Apply Classification Algorithms

The model first generates association rules using Apriori Algorithm and calculates accuracy. The test is performed 10 times to get an average of accuracy. After that a set of classification algorithms is tested and results are calculated. The algorithms include Naïve Bayes, NN, VQNN, OWANN, J48, FuzzyNN, FONN and algorithms. The details of these algorithms is given in proposed model chapter.

For example purposes, cluster C1 is chosen. The model first generates association rules using Apriori Algorithm for the cluster, and calculates accuracy. The test is performed10 times and an average of accuracy is calculated. Now, *Make* is predicted by using top-ranked variables with the help of different classification algorithms. The prediction is done by creating an ARFF file for Weka Tool and 10-fold cross validation is used in the process. Advanced measures of evaluation like Accuracy, Time Consumption, Recall, Precision and F-Measure for each algorithm are also calculated. The results of these measures are passed to the next step for evaluation purposes.

4.2.3.2 Evaluate Using Advanced Measures

Once the results are ready, these results are passed to this step for advanced evaluation. This step allows the evaluation of algorithm based upon Accuracy, Recall, Precision and F-Measures. A review of these measures is provided in the previous chapter. This step also involves the visualization component which strengthens the process as well as enables the selection of an algorithm in better way. The visualization component allows the visualization of one algorithm at once. It involves a graphical display of Accuracy, Precision, Recall, and F-Measures along with the support to see the values in a tabular format. The table contains values for these measures along with the time taken in model building in milliseconds.

For the cluster C1, model predicts *Make* by using top-ranked variables with the help of the above mentioned algorithms. The results of the discussed measures above are given in the Table 7. The results are passed to the visualization component which generates a graph to show the advanced

Table 7. Evaluation results of algorithms using 3-top ranked variables for prediction

Algorithm	Accuracy	Time (ms)	Recall	Precision	F-Measure
NN	39.4161%	0.09	0.394	0.336	0.343
VQNN	39.4161%	0.01	0.394	0.34	0.344
OWANN	37.2263%	0.011	0.372	0.341	0.334
J 48	52.5547%	0.2	0.526	0.471	0.462
FuzzyNN	2.9197%	0.002	0.029	0.022	0.024
FONN	48.1752%	0.001	0.482	0.465	0.451
Naïve Bayes	45.9854%	0.01	0.46	0.451	0.408
Apriori	41.96%	1.5	-	-	-

Figure 9. Visualization of Naïve Bayes classifier against advanced measures for cluster C1

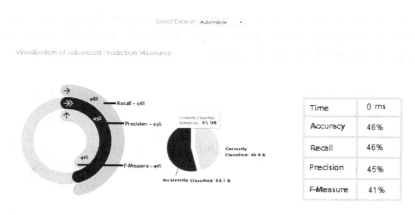

measures for the user for analysis purposes as shown in the Figure 9. The left hand side of the visualization component shows advanced measures called Recall, Precision and F-Measure which makes it easier for the analyst to review. The middle section of the visualization component is shows the percentage of correctly and incorrectly classified instances based on the accuracy measure. The measures are shown in tabular format on right side of the visualization component.

4.2.3.3 Predict Using Selected Algorithm

The last step of this process allows the selection of an algorithm from previous step and proceeds to prediction of the unknown instances based on the selected algorithm. The selection is based upon the values of advanced measures used in the model including Accuracy, Recall, Precision and F-Measure. The model also calculates Time for building the model which can also be considered for evaluation. For the example, the best suited algorithm is J48 which provides highest values for all measures except it takes a little more time for model building than other algorithms.

4.2.4 Prediction of Numeric Variable

Likewise, if the variable to be predicted in a numeric variable the model adapts Path P2. This path is also a series of steps. It takes ranking of variables as input along with the cluster data from the previous stage like prediction of nominal variable. In the first step the process creates a STAR schema and then applies classification algorithms to gather results. These algorithms are evaluated using advanced measures in the next step like before to select a particular algorithm. In the last step actual prediction is done using the selected algorithm.

4.2.4.1 Generate STAR Schema

The input for this step is the cluster and top ranked variables. These variables are used to generate a STAR schema which is exploited further for prediction purposes. The schema generation process is same as described in the pattern extraction module. For the example dataset, the STAR schema is generated as shown in Figure 10. For example purposes, all dimensions are used in the schema as this schema will also be used for aggregate facts prediction in a data warehouse environment. But due to lack of space, only few dimension tables are shown.

4.2.4.2 Apply Classification Algorithms

This step takes the STAR schema generated in the previous step as input and applies classification algorithms on it. The classification algorithms include Multi Layer Perceptron, Linear Regression and Simple Linear Regression since the predicted variable is numeric in this case. A review of these algorithms is already presented in previous section.

For the implementation of this step, the data is passed to WEKA tool like before and classification algorithms are applied. The variable *Normalized Losses* is predicted using the top-ranked variables (*City MPG, Highway-MPG and Height*). The evaluation measures are calculated for each of the algorithm for evaluation in the next step.

4.2.4.3 Evaluate Using Advanced Measures

After the classification algorithms are applied, the evaluation is done using measures namely Correlation Coefficient (CC), Mean absolute error (MSE), and Root mean squared error (RMSE). A review of these measures is presented in the previous section. For the example cluster, these measures are calculated

Figure 10. Multidimensional schema for cluster C1 to predict numeric variables

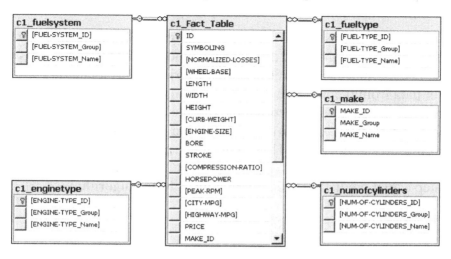

against each algorithm in the previous step. The values retrieved through the process are shown in the Table 8. The table provides these measures against all algorithms used for the prediction of *Normalized Losses*.

4.2.4.4 Predict Using Selected Algorithm

The last step of this process allows the selection of an algorithm from previous step and proceeds to prediction of the unknown instances based on the selected algorithm. The selection is based upon the values of advanced measures used in the model including Correlation Coefficient (CC), Mean absolute error (MSE), and Root mean squared error (RMSE). For the example cluster, the best suited algorithm is Simple Linear Regression. The Correlation Coefficient confirms that the prediction pattern is better and error rates MAE and RMSE are also lesser than the other models.

Table 8. Evaluation results of algorithms using 3-top ranked variables for prediction

Algorithm	CC	MAE	RMSE
Multilayer Perceptron	0.396	0.117	0.1844
Simple Linear Regression	0.6666	0.0794	0.1343
Linear Regression	0.663	0.0877	0.1351

CC = Correlation Coefficient, MAE = Mean Absolute Error, RMSE = Root Mean Squared Error

4.2.5 Prediction of Aggregate Data

The model also allows the prediction of aggregate data available in a multi-dimensional environment. In this case the model adapts Path P3. This path is also a series of steps. It takes ranking of variables as input along with the cluster data from the previous stage like prediction of aggregate data in the multi-dimensional environment. In the first step the process creates a STAR schema, generates data cube on top of the schema and then applies classification algorithms to gather results. These algorithms are evaluated using advanced measures in the next step like before to select a particular algorithm. In the last step actual prediction is done using the selected algorithm.

4.2.5.1 Generate STAR Schema

In this step, the process generates a STAR schema by using all variables. The numeric variables are taken as facts where as nominal variables are taken as dimensions. A dimension table is created against each of the nominal variables and a foreign key is created to link the fact table and dimension table. For the example purposes, the schema is generated for cluster C1 which is same as in the previous section.

4.2.5.2 Compute Data Cube

Once the STAR schema is ready, the model computes a data cube on the schema by importing all data from the cluster to this schema. The resultant data cube contains data in aggregate form. For example purposes, data of cluster C1 is imported in the data warehouse. Some sample data from the data cube is showing in Table 9. The numeric columns present the data in Average aggregate measure.

Table 9. 5 records sample from data cube for the schema of cluster C1

Make	Fuel Type	Aspiration	No. of Doors	Body Style	Symboling	Losses	Wheel Base	Length	Width	Horse Power
audi	gas	turbo	four	sedan	0.6	0.49	0.56	0.77	0.92	0.38
toyota	gas	turbo	two	hatchback	1	0.46	0.27	0.48	0.5	0.17
honda	gas	std	two	hatchback	0.4	0.21	0.29	0.39	0.41	0.17
toyota	gas	std	four	hatchback	0.4	0.14	0.27	0.38	0.34	0.35
toyota	gas	turbo	two	hatchback	1	0.05	0.27	0.48	0.5	0.22

4.2.5.3 Apply Classification Algorithms

This step takes the data cube generated in the previous step as input and applies classification algorithms on it. The classification algorithms include Multi-Layer Perceptron, Linear Regression and Simple Linear Regression.

For the implementation of this step, the data cube generated in the previous step is taken as example and classification algorithms are applied. These algorithms predict Average *Length* with the help of *Aspiration, Body Style* and *Average Wheel Base*. The evaluation measures are calculated for each of the algorithm for evaluation in the next step.

4.2.5.4 Evaluate Using Advanced Measures

After the classification algorithms are applied, the evaluation is done using measures namely Correlation Coefficient (CC), Mean absolute error (MSE), and Root mean squared error (RMSE). For the example data, these measures are calculated against each algorithm in the previous step. The values retrieved through the process are shown in the Table 10. The table provides these measures against all algorithms used for the prediction of Average *Length* using the variables *Aspiration, Body Style* and *Average Wheel Base*.

4.2.5.5 Predict Using Selected Algorithm

The last step of this process allows the selection of an algorithm from previous step and proceeds to prediction of the unknown instances based on the selected algorithm. The selection is based upon the values of advanced measures used in the model including Correlation Coefficient (CC), Mean absolute error (MSE), and Root mean squared error (RMSE). For the example, the best suited algorithm is Linear Regression. The Correlation Coefficient confirms that the prediction pattern is better and error rates MAE and RMSE are also lesser than the other models.

Table 10. Evaluation results of algorithms using to predict Horse Power Variable

Algorithm	CC	MAE	RMSE
Multilayer Perceptron	0.8869	0.0423	0.0851
Simple Linear Regression	0.8100	0.0301	0.0694
Linear Regression	0.9136	0.0359	0.0737

CC = Correlation Coefficient, MAE = Mean Absolute Error, RMSE = Root Mean Squared Error

4.3 SUMMARY

In this chapter, the proposed model has been implemented on the *Automobile* dataset. The pattern extraction module has been explained by taking a cluster on second layer, and by extracting association rules from it with the methodology discussed above in detail. This component now only allows the extraction but doesn't involve the user in the process, allows automatic generation of schema at different levels, uses advanced measures of evaluation and provides a mean for the users to visualize the results. The pattern prediction component provides ability to select classification model that fits the data, with the help of a series of steps explained above. This component has the ability to apply multiple algorithms at once, and evaluate these based on advanced measures. The evaluation process also includes a visualization component to assist the user to select a particular algorithm for prediction purposes. Since this dataset contains very small number of records, the next chapter includes the experimental study on a larger dataset called *Adult* taken from UCI Machine Learning website.

REFERENCES

Asuncion, A., & Newman, D. (2007). *UCI machine learning repository.* Academic Press.

Rosario, G. E., Rundensteiner, E. A., Brown, D. C., Ward, M. O., & Huang, S. (2004). Mapping nominal values to numbers for effective visualization. *Information Visualization*, *3*(2), 80–95. doi:10.1057/palgrave.ivs.9500072

Usman, M., Pears, R., & Fong, A. C. M. (2013). Discovering diverse association rules from multidimensional schema. *Expert Systems with Applications*, *40*(15), 5975–5996. doi:10.1016/j.eswa.2013.05.031

Chapter 5
Experimental Study II:
Adult Dataset

ABSTRACT

This chapter provides an experimental study of the proposed model on Adult data set. The chapter includes the implementation of pattern extraction from this dataset by following a series of steps as discussed before. It also includes detailed implementation of pattern prediction of numeric variables, nominal variables, and aggregate data. The implementation of pattern prediction is also a series of steps as discussed before.

5.1 DATASET INTRODUCTION

Adult dataset is taken from UCI machine learning repository (Asuncion & Newman, 2007). The data set has a mixture of numerical and nominal type of variables (13 in total). The whole data set contains 48,842 records. Eight variables of the dataset are nominal and rest five variables are numeric. Nominal variables along with their distinct values are given in Table 1. The numeric variables include *Age, Final Weight, Edu Num, Cap Gain, Cap Loss, Hrs Per Week*. Since the available data set contains missing values, we removed records with missing values and used 61% of the total records (30,162) for our case study.

DOI: 10.4018/978-1-5225-5029-7.ch005

5.2 PATTERN EXTRACTION

This section presents the first part of the proposed framework called Pattern Extraction. As discussed above, this part works through a series of steps where each step takes input from the previous step. The steps involve hierarchical clusters generation, ranking of variables, multi-dimensional scaling, schema generation, mining of association rules, advanced evaluation of association rules and visualization of extracted patterns. The sub sections below explain each step briefly and then provide implementation using the example dataset.

5.2.1 Generate Hierarchical Clusters

In the first step of the model, *Agglomerative Hierarchical Clustering* is applied to all data based on numerical variables to generate clusters at different levels in the hierarchy. A detailed discussion of this step has already been provided in the proposed model chapter. This step produces clusters which are numbered manually at each level and presented using a tree structure in Figure 1. Cluster C11 is highlighted in green, as further mining is done on this cluster as detailed in upcoming sections.

Table 1. Nominal variables along with their distinct values from adults dataset

Nominal Variable	Distinct Values
Work Class	Private, Self-emp-not-inc, Self-emp-inc, Federal-gov, Local-gov, State-gov, Without-pay, Never-worked
Education	Bachelors, Some-college, 11th, HS-grad, Prof-school, Assoc-acdm, Assoc-voc, 9th, 7th-8th, 12th, Masters, 1st-4th, 10th, Doctorate, 5th-6th, Preschool
Marital Status	Married-civ-spouse, Divorced, Never-married, Separated, Widowed, Married-spouse-absent, Married-AF-spouse
Occupation	Tech-support, Craft-repair, Other-service, Sales, Exec-managerial, Prof-specialty, Handlers-cleaners, Machine-op-inspct, Adm-clerical, Farming-fishing, Transport-moving, Priv-house-serv, Protective-serv, Armed-Forces
Relationship	Wife, Own-child, Husband, Not-in-family, Other-relative, Unmarried
Race	White, Asian-Pac-Islander, Amer-Indian-Eskimo, Other, Black
Sex	Female, Male
Native Country	United-States, Cambodia, England, Puerto-Rico, Canada, Germany, Outlying-US(Guam-USVI-etc), India, Japan, Greece, South, China, Cuba, Iran, Honduras, Philippines, Italy, Poland, Jamaica, Vietnam, Mexico, Portugal, Ireland, France, Dominican-Republic, Laos, Ecuador, Taiwan, Haiti, Columbia, Hungary, Guatemala, Nicaragua, Scotland, Thailand, Yugoslavia, El-Salvador, Trinadad&Tobago, Peru, Hong, Holand-Netherlands

5.2.2 Rank Variables

After the dendrogram is created, the model applies Principal Component Analysis to rank the variables within each cluster. However since PCA only works on numeric data, the model applies another technique to convert nominal data into the numeric data to apply PCA. The model takes data of all nominal variables and converts it to numeric values using Rosarios's Approach(Rosario, Rundensteiner, Brown, Ward, & Huang, 2004). A detailed discussion on this approach has already been provided in the proposed model chapter.

5.2.2.1 Convert Nominal Variables to Numeric Variables

To convert nominal variables to numeric variables, input files for the cluster are prepared for the tool used for this method and conversion is performed. The quantified versions of selected variables in a Parallel Coordinates display are shown in Figure 2 for cluster C11.

In parallel coordinates, each vertical line represents one variable, and each polyline cutting across the vertical axes represents instances in the dataset. The nominal variables

Work Class, Sex, Education and *Occupation* are shown using vertical lines, where as distinct values with order and spacing are shown on the vertical lines. The variables are ordered such that the vertical axes of highly associated variables are positioned next to each other for easier interpretation. The semantic relationship is clear between nominal variables through polylines in the diagram. Once the process is completed, all data of the clusters is available in numeric format.

Figure 1. Tree structure of hierarchical clusters

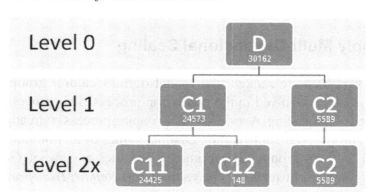

Figure 2. Quantification display of Rossario's approach in parallel coordinates for cluster C11

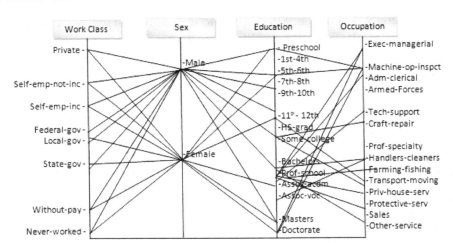

5.2.2.2 Apply Principal Component Analysis (PCA)

After the data is available in the numeric format, Principal Component Analysis is applied in order to measure the degree of variance for each variable and rank variables in the clusters. A detailed discussion on PCA has already been provided in proposed model chapter. Figure 3 shows the ranking of numeric variables in the three clusters after performing the PCA where as nominal variable ranking is shown in Figure 4.

It is evident from the Figures 3 and 4 that the list of nominal variables is unique across the clusters however the numerical variables list is not unique. The C1 and C11 clusters have the same number of variables, whereas C12 cluster has some variables which have zero variance and these are not used in the ranking process by SPSS.

5.2.3 Apply Multi-Dimensional Scaling

After the variables are ranked, the model defines natural grouping of all nominal variables involved in the prediction process. This process is called multi-dimensional scaling. A review of the grouping process is already provided in detail in proposed model chapter. Distinct values of all nominal variables are joined to form groups. The Figure 5 provides a view of *Occupation* variables groups in cluster C11. The values *Craft-Repair, Transport-Moving,*

Figure 3. Ranking of numeric variables using PCA for clusters C1, C11 and C12

C1		
Variable Name	**Calculated Value**	**Rank**
EDU_NUM	0.63	1
HRS_PER_WEEK	0.46	2
AGE	0.33	3
CAP_LOSS	0.29	4
CAP_GAIN	0.20	5
FNL_WGT	-0.16	6

C11		
Variable Name	**Calculated Value**	**Rank**
EDU_NUM	0.67	1
HRS_PER_WEEK	0.45	2
CAP_LOSS	0.29	3
AGE	0.28	4
CAP_GAIN	0.20	5
FNL_WGT	-0.20	6

C12		
Variable Name	**Calculated Value**	**Rank**
EDU_NUM	0.70	1
HRS_PER_WEEK	0.49	2
AGE	0.38	3
FNL_WGT	0.11	4

Figure 4. Ranking of nominal variables using PCA for clusters C1, C11 and C12

C1		
Variable Name	**Calculated Value**	**Rank**
SEX	0.56	1
OCCUPATION	0.39	2
WORK_CLASS	-0.01	3
EDUCATION	-0.01	4
COUNTRY	-0.25	5
RACE	-0.25	6
RELATIONSHIP	-0.89	7
MARITAL_STATUS	-0.89	8

C11		
Variable Name	**Calculated Value**	**Rank**
SEX	0.56	1
OCCUPATION	0.35	2
WORK_CLASS	0.04	3
RACE	-0.09	4
COUNTRY	-0.11	5
EDUCATION	-0.17	6
RELATIONSHIP	-0.93	7
MARITAL_STATUS	-0.93	8

C12		
Variable Name	**Calculated Value**	**Rank**
RELATIONSHIP	0.87	1
MARITAL_STATUS	0.87	2
SEX	0.66	3
OCCUPATION	0.53	4
WORK_CLASS	0.34	5
RACE	0.29	6
COUNTRY	0.24	7
EDUCATION	0.10	8

Figure 5. Multidimensional schema of adults dataset for cluster C11

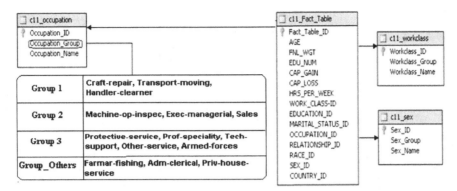

and *Handler-Cleaners* show closeness with each other and therefore grouped together in a single group. The Group-Others is obtained by including all other values with no similarities with each other. Such grouping is hard to obtain in case of manual work. All nominal variable groups are obtained and input in a separate work sheet.

It is clear from the group information that occupation values are naturally grouped together. For example, the persons having Craft-Repair, Transport-Moving and Handler-Cleaner occupation values are generated tend to be closely related due to their behavior and there for these are grouped together. Similarly other dimensions such as *Work Class*, *Relationship* and *Marital Status* etc also contain groupings which enlighten the semantic relationship present in these variables.

5.2.4 Generate STAR Schema

After grouping has been obtained, the model takes nominal variables as dimensions and numeric variables as facts to create a multidimensional STAR schema. A review of STAR schema has been given in proposed model chapter. This schema generation process is based on algorithms 1,2 as discussed in the same chapter. We create multidimensional schema using top ranked variables. An example of multidimensional schema is given in Figure 5 which displays the schema for cluster C11. The schema contains a fact table with name C11_Fact_Table. The top ranked dimensions were used to create three dimension tables: C11_WorkClass, C11_Occupation and C11_Sex. The fact table contains all numeric columns as facts and all dimension names as foreign keys to the respective dimension tables.

5.2.5 Mine Association Rules

After the schema is generated and data is in the data warehouse, the model extracts patterns in the form of association rules. A detailed discussion on association rule mining has already been provided in the proposed model chapter. Association rule mining is applied on original data within clusters as well as using the multidimensional schema for that cluster. Association rule mining is performed for cluster C11 using the schema generated through proposed method and the results are shown in Table 2. This table shows the top 10 extracted patterns from cluster C11. These results are helpful for the analyst to get an abstract review of the cluster. Like in the previous case study, the rules are compared with the approach of (Usman, Pears, & Fong, 2013). The rules generated from the approach in (Usman et al., 2013) are shown in the Table 3. It is clear that proposed approach provides better importance. It is evident that proposed approach provides more important rules than the approach in (Usman et al., 2013). Top ranked rule in previous approach has importance value 0.57 whereas proposed approach provides top ranked rule with important value of 0.95.

5.2.6 Evaluate Association Rules Using Advance Measures

Once the rules are obtained, these are evaluated using advanced measures. As described in the example data set in previous chapter that extracted

Table 2. Rule generated from proposed methodology for cluster C11

Rules	Imp.
1. Occupation Group =Group3,Sex Group=Group-Others→Work Class Name =Local-gov	0.95
2. Occupation Group = Group 3 → WORKCLASS Name =Local-gov	0.95
3. Occupation Group =Group3, Sex Group =Group-Others→Work Class Name=Local-gov	0.83
4. Occupation Group=Group-Others, Sex Group=Group-Others→ WorkClass Name = Private	0.11
5. Occupation Group = Group-Others → Work Class Name =Private	0.11
6. Occupation Group = Group 3 → Work Class Name =Private	0.11
7. Occupation Group =Group 3, Sex Group =Group-Others→ Work Class Name =Private	0.11
8. Occupation Group =Group 3, Sex Group =Group-Others→ Work Class Name =Private	0.10
9. Occupation Group = Group-Others → Work Class Name =Private	0.09
10. Occupation Name=Group-Others, Sex Group =Group-Others→Workclass Name =Private	0.09

Table 3. Rules generated from the methodology proposed by (Usman et al., 2013)

Rules	Imp.
1. Education Group=Group3,Occupation Group=group2 →Relationship Name=Own-child	0.57
2. Education Group=group3, Occupation Group=group2→ Relationship Name=Own-child	0.57
3. Education Group=group3, Occupation Group=group3→ Relationship Name=Own-child	0.51
4. Education Group=group3, Occupation Group=group1→ Relationship Name=Own-child	0.42
5. Education Group=group3, Occupation Group=group4→ Relationship Name=Own-child	0.40
6. Education Group = group3 → Relationship Name = Own-child	0.39
7. Education Group=group3, Occupation Group=group3→ Relationship Name=Own-child	0.38
8. Education Group=group3, Occupation Group=group3→ Relationship Name=Own-child	0.37
9. Education Grp.=group3, Occupation Grp=group_others→ Relationship Name=Own-child	0.36
10. Education Group=group2, Occupation Group=group1→ Relationship Name= Husband	0.32

patterns must be validated with advanced measures in order to measure the interestingness for the user, diversity measures called Rae, CON, and Hill measures are applied on extracted patterns. Same calculations are done for non-schema rules. It is evident that the diversity values are greater for schema rules in all cases. The results are shown in Table 4. Similar results of previous approach are shown in Table 5. The increase achieved in diversity between rules generated from schema and without schema is calculated in both approaches. The comparison of proposed approach and approach in (Usman et al., 2013) is given in Figures 6, 7 and 8. Figure 6 presents the comparison of diversity increase (%) for Rae measure. It is evident that the increase in diversity between non-schema and schema rule sets is very prominent than the approach adapted by(Usman et al., 2013). Similarly proposed approach yields better increase for other measures (CON, Hill) as depicted in Figures 7 and 8.

5.2.7 Visualize Association Rules

The mining process discussed in the previous steps allows the mining of association rules from large datasets. The process is also assisted by a visualization component. The generated rules are visualized using a graphical interface in order to assist the analysts in the mining process. The interface contains two components. The first one is called "Clusters + Rule Sets". In Figure 9, the C11 cluster has been visualized in first component. The left side shows the clusters in the dataset, and C11 is chosen to visualize. On

Table 4. Comparison of diversity measures between rules with schema and without schema rules in proposed approach

Clusters	Rule Set	Rae		CON		Hill	
		No Schema	With Schema	No Schema	With Schema	No Schema	With Schema
C1	R1-R6	0.178	**0.338**	0.115	**0.453**	-4.484	**-1.636**
	R1-R7	0.157	**0.295**	0.127	**0.422**	-5.157	**-1.949**
	R1-R8	0.140	**0.278**	0.131	**0.418**	-5.840	**-2.096**
	R1-R9	0.123	**0.271**	0.115	**0.424**	-6.831	**-2.159**
	R1-R10	0.110	**0.264**	0.103	**0.427**	-7.785	**-2.217**
C11	R1-R6	0.178	**0.366**	0.115	**0.489**	-4.488	**-1.325**
	R1-R7	0.157	**0.279**	0.127	**0.399**	-5.159	**-2.032**
	R1-R8	0.140	**0.218**	0.131	**0.326**	-5.833	**-3.013**
	R1-R9	0.130	**0.213**	0.146	**0.338**	-6.286	**-3.093**
	R1-R10	0.120	**0.208**	0.148	**0.346**	-6.861	**-3.167**
C12	R1-R6	0.260	**0.362**	0.384	**0.487**	-2.201	**-1.578**
	R1-R7	0.211	**0.335**	0.324	**0.476**	-3.042	**-1.738**
	R1-R8	0.191	**0.330**	0.315	**0.487**	-3.377	**-1.767**
	R1-R9	0.173	**0.303**	0.305	**0.468**	-3.721	**-1.961**
	R1-R10	0.158	**0.301**	0.294	**0.476**	-4.072	**-1.976**

right side, the tool displays the rules sets based upon the size selected. The interface shows rule sets based on Rae and Con values on x and y axis. The average importance of a particular rule set decides on the size of the bubble in the chart. We provide detailed information on hover of a particular rule set including all advanced measures like *Rae, Con, Hill* and *Importance*.

After a specific rule set is selected to be explored further for rules inside, the user is shown the second tab called "Association Rules". The second tab is shown in Figure 10. The left side of this tab shows all rules in the rule set. User is able to select the rule on left side to view more detailed information of the rule included the actual rule, its support, confidence, importance and probability on right side. The interface also allows user to review the grouping information of the variables involved on left side. In this case, Rule # 2 is being reviewed, which shows detailed information on right side. This information includes the rule details along with values of importance, support and confidence. Since the left hand side of the rule contains two variables *Occupation* and *Sex*, the grouping information against these variables is shown at the bottom. User can review any rule set like this along with its details.

119

Table 5. Comparison of diversity measures between rules with schema and without schema rules in previous approach

Clusters	Rule Set	Rae		CON		Hill	
		No Schema	With Schema	No Schema	With Schema	No Schema	With Schema
C1	R1-R6	0.322	**0.337**	0.432	**0.452**	-1.693	**-1.636**
	R1-R7	0.259	**0.295**	0.369	**0.421**	-2.302	**-1.948**
	R1-R8	0.218	**0.277**	0.327	**0.418**	-2.873	**-2.095**
	R1-R9	0.204	**0.27**	0.325	**0.423**	-3.084	**-2.159**
	R1-R10	0.192	**0.264**	0.321	**0.427**	-3.285	**-2.216**
C11	R1-R6	0.322	**0.397**	0.432	**0.526**	-1.693	**-1.286**
	R1-R7	0.256	**0.376**	0.365	**0.522**	-2.346	**-1.385**
	R1-R8	0.216	**0.312**	0.324	**0.463**	-2.918	**-1.805**
	R1-R9	0.204	**0.309**	0.325	**0.472**	-3.084	**-1.829**
	R1-R10	0.192	**0.303**	0.321	**0.475**	-3.285	**-1.872**
C12	R1-R6	0.164	**0.263**	0.263	**0.371**	-3.017	**-2.248**
	R1-R7	0.217	**0.312**	0.353	**0.454**	-2.437	**-1.703**
	R1-R8	0.172	**0.297**	0.294	**0.454**	-3.339	**-1.8**
	R1-R9	0.142	**0.279**	0.252	**0.441**	-4.261	**-2.11**
	R1-R10	0.136	**0.276**	0.448	**0.443**	-4.755	**-2.141**

Figure 6. Comparison of % increase in diversity (Rae) of our approach and approach proposed by (Usman et al., 2013)

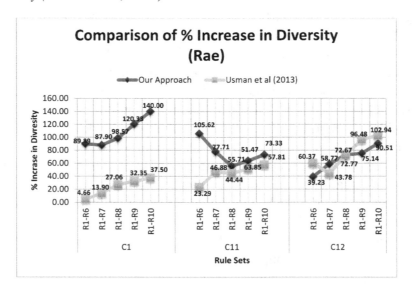

Figure 7. Comparison of % Increase in diversity (CON) of our approach and approach proposed by (Usman et al., 2013)

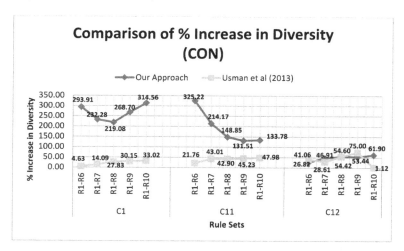

Figure 8. Comparison of % increase in diversity (Hill) of our approach and approach proposed by (Usman et al., 2013)

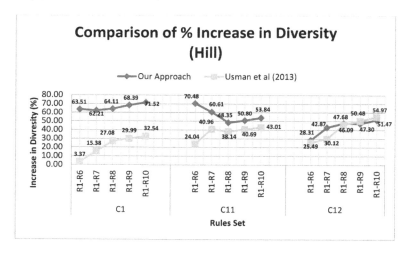

5.3 PATTERN PREDICTION

This section presents the second module of the proposed framework called Pattern Prediction. As discussed in previous chapter, this module works through a series of steps where each step takes input from the previous step. The process starts by obtaining hierarchical clusters and ranking of variables.

Figure 9. Visualization of pattern extraction process of cluster C11 (Component 1)

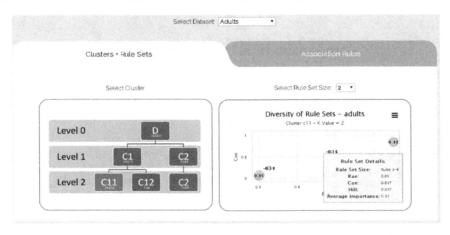

Figure 10. Visualization of pattern extraction process of cluster C11 (Component 2)

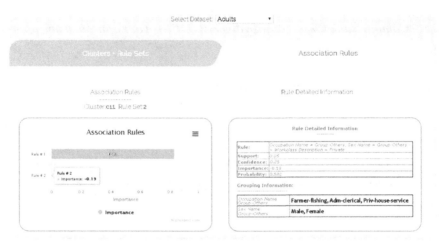

After ranking, Path P1, P2 and P3 are adapted to derive a classification model, which is evaluated in the next step. The selection of path depends upon the nature of variable being predicted. After evaluation, a model is selected to predict the patterns.

5.3.1 Generate Hierarchical Clusters

The first step in pattern prediction involves hierarchical clusters generation like pattern extraction. The step creates clusters at different levels in the hierarchy for further mining purposes. The hierarchical clustering mechanism has already been discussed in detail in pattern extraction section of previous chapter. For pattern prediction, previous clustering results are used.

5.3.2 Rank Variables

Once the clusters are obtained, the ranking process is started to rank variables. In this component, a different process of ranking the available variables is adapted. This ranking process is based on normality of variables as discussed previously. Normality curves are drawn for each of the variable in each cluster and top ranked variables are picked. If a variable contains data which satisfies normality better than the other variables, it is considered to have more effect on classification. The ranking results are given in Figure 11. It is clear that, in C1, *Occupation, Education and Relationship* are ranked on top and thus can be used to generated classification rules of this particular cluster (keeping in view the *Work Class* is the variable to predict).

Figure 11. Ranking of C1, C11, and C12 clusters. Nominal Variables are shown by a +

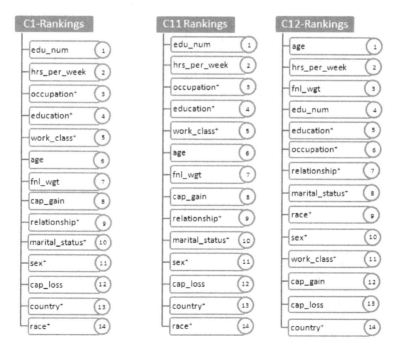

5.3.3 Prediction of Nominal Variable

If the variable to be predicted in a nominal variable the model adapts Path P1. This path is a series of steps. It takes ranking of variables as input along with the cluster data. In the first step classification algorithms are applied and results are gathered. These algorithms are evaluated using advanced measures in the next step to select a particular algorithm. In the last step actual prediction is done using the selected algorithm.

5.3.3.1 Apply Classification Algorithms

The model first generates association rules using Apriori Algorithm and calculates accuracy. The test is performed 10 times to get an average of accuracy. After that a set of classification algorithms is tested and results are calculated. The algorithms include Naïve Bayes, NN, VQNN, OWANN, J48, FuzzyNN, FONN and algorithms. The details of these algorithms are given in proposed model chapter.

For example purposes, cluster C11 is chosen. The model first generates association rules using Apriori Algorithm for the cluster, and calculates accuracy. The test is performed 10 times and an average of accuracy is calculated. Now, *Work Class* is predicted by using top-ranked variables with the help of different classification algorithms. The prediction is done by creating an ARFF file for Weka Tool and 10-fold cross validation is used in the process. Advanced measures of evaluation like Accuracy, Time Consumption, Recall, Precision and F-Measure for each algorithm are also calculated. The time taken to build each classification model using top-ranked variables is also calculated. The classification models are run again by using all variables for prediction to draw a comparison. The results are passed to the next step for evaluation purposes.

5.3.3.2 Evaluate Using Advanced Measures

Once the results are ready, these results are passed to this step for advanced evaluation. This step allows the evaluation of algorithm based upon Accuracy, Recall, Precision and F-Measures. A review of these measures is provided in the proposed model chapter. This step also involves the visualization component which strengthens the process as well as enables the selection of an algorithm in better way. The visualization component allows the visualization of one algorithm at once. It involves a graphical display of Accuracy, Precision, Recall, and F-Measures along with the support to see the values in a tabular format. The table contains values for these measures along with the time taken in model building in milliseconds.

For cluster C11, the results calculated in the previous step are given in Table 6. Same results are shown in Figure 13 where an algorithm can be visualized for all the measures calculated in the table. The left hand side of the visualization component shows advanced measures called Recall, Precision and F-Measure which makes it easier for the analyst to review. The middle section of the visualization component shows the percentage of correctly and incorrectly classified instances based on the accuracy measure. The measures are shown in a tabular format on right side of the visualization component. Moreover, the time consumption in case of selected variables and all variables is also compared in the Table 7 and Figure 12. The results not only show that selection of variables has a big impact on time consumption. But it also allows the user to compare all algorithms based on time consumption at once.

5.3.3.3 Predict Using Selected Algorithm

The last step of this process allows the selection of an algorithm from previous step and proceeds to prediction of the unknown instances based on the selected algorithm. The selection is based upon the values of advanced measures used in the model including Accuracy, Recall, Precision and F-Measure. The model also calculates Time for building the model which can also be considered for evaluation. For the example, the best suited algorithm is J48 which provides highest values for all measures except it takes a little more time for model building than other algorithms.

Table 6. Evaluation of algorithms using 3-top ranked variables for prediction C11

Algorithm	Accuracy	Time (ms)	Recall	Precision	F-Measure
NN	76.43 %	80	0.764	0.675	0.7
VQNN	76.43 %	60	0.764	0.675	0.7
OWANN	76.49%	40	0.762	0.673	0.7
J 48	77.33%	1320	0.773	0.696	0.698
FuzzyNN	76.43 %	40	0.764	0.59	0.664
FONN	76.32%	80	0.763	0.675	0.701
Naïve Bayes	76.73%	110	0.767	0.706	0.708
Apriori	64.60%	-	-	-	-

Table 7. Comparison time of different algorithms in adult data set using all variables and top-ranked variables for cluster C11

	NN	VQNN	OWANN	J 48	FuzzyNN	FONN	Naïve Bayes
All Variables	90	110	110	3390	100	90	110
Selected Variables	80	60	40	1320	40	80	110

Figure 12. Comparison of time (ms) required to build the model using all variables and using top-ranked variables for cluster C11

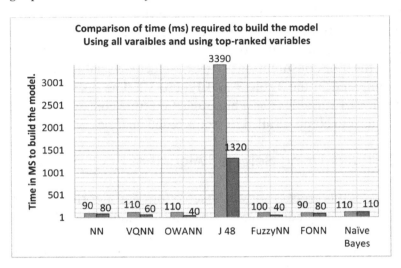

Figure 13. Visualization of Naïve Bayes classifier against advanced measures

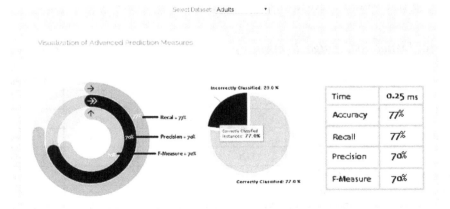

5.3.4 Prediction of Numeric Variable

Likewise, if the variable to be predicted in a numeric variable the model adapts Path P2. This path is also a series of steps. It takes ranking of variables as input along with the cluster data from the previous stage like prediction of nominal variable. In the first step the process creates a STAR schema and then applies classification algorithms to gather results. These algorithms are evaluated using advanced measures in the next step like before to select a particular algorithm. In the last step actual prediction is done using the selected algorithm.

5.3.4.1 Generate STAR Schema

The input for this step is the cluster and top ranked variables. These variables are used to generate a STAR schema which is exploited further for prediction purposes. The schema generation process is same as described in the pattern extraction module. For the example dataset, the STAR schema is generated as shown in Figure 14. For example purposes, all dimensions are used in the schema as this schema will also be used for aggregate facts prediction in a data warehouse environment.

Figure 14. Multidimensional schema for cluster C11 to predict numeric variables

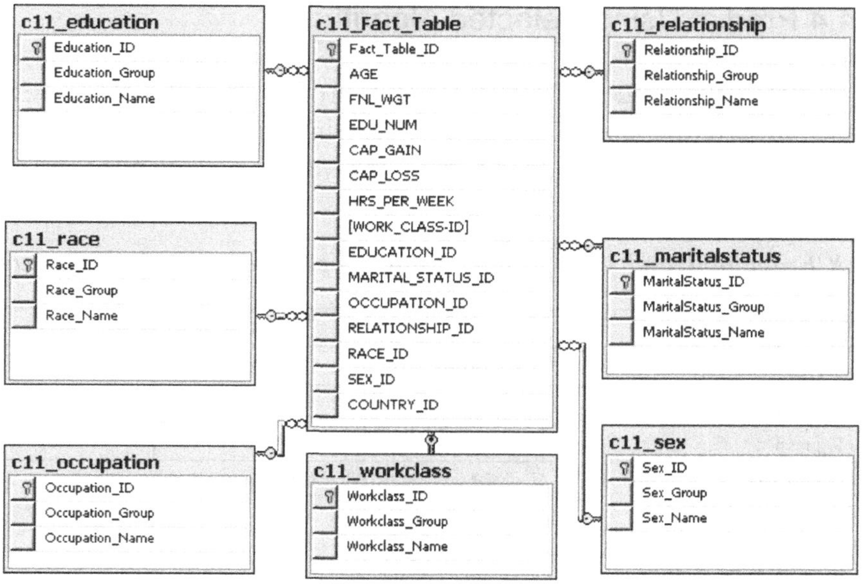

5.3.4.2 Apply Classification Algorithms

This step takes the STAR schema generated in the previous step as input and applies classification algorithms on it. The classification algorithms include Multi Layer Perceptron, Linear Regression and Simple Linear Regression since the predicted variable is numeric in this case. A review of these algorithms is already presented in previous section.

For the implementation of this step, the data for cluster C11 is passed to WEKA tool like before and classification algorithms are applied. The variable *Cap Gain* is predicted using the top-ranked variables (*Edu Num, Hrs Per Week and age*). The evaluation measures are calculated for each of the algorithm for evaluation in the next step.

5.3.4.3 Evaluate Using Advanced Measures

After the classification algorithms are applied, the evaluation is done using measures namely Correlation Coefficient (CC), Mean absolute error (MSE), and Root mean squared error (RMSE). A review of these measures is presented in the previous section. For the example cluster, these measures are calculated against each algorithm in the previous step. The values retrieved through the process are shown in the Table 8. The table provides these measures against all algorithms used for the prediction of *Cap Gain*.

5.3.4.4 Predict Using Selected Algorithm

The last step of this process allows the selection of an algorithm from previous step and proceeds to prediction of the unknown instances based on the selected algorithm. The selection is based upon the values of advanced measures

Table 8. Evaluation results of algorithms using 3-top ranked variables for prediction

Algorithm	CC	MAE	RMSE
Multilayer Perceptron	0.0866	0.0108	0.0236
Simple Linear Regression	0.1528	0.0097	0.0228
Linear Regression	0.1905	0.0097	0.0226

CC = Correlation Coefficient, MAE = Mean Absolute Error, RMSE = Root Mean Squared Error

used in the model including Correlation Coefficient (CC), Mean absolute error (MSE), and Root mean squared error (RMSE). For the example cluster, the best suited algorithm is Linear Regression. The Correlation Coefficient confirms that the prediction pattern is better and error rates MAE and RMSE are also lesser than the other models.

5.3.5 Prediction of Aggregate Data

The model also allows the prediction of aggregate data available in a multi-dimensional environment. In this case the model adapts Path P3. This path is also a series of steps. It takes ranking of variables as input along with the cluster data from the previous stage like prediction of aggregate data in the multi-dimensional environment. In the first step the process creates a STAR schema, generates data cube on top of the schema and then applies classification algorithms to gather results. These algorithms are evaluated using advanced measures in the next step like before to select a particular algorithm. In the last step actual prediction is done using the selected algorithm.

5.3.5.1 Generate STAR Schema

In this step, the process generates a STAR schema by using all variables. The numeric variables are taken as facts where as nominal variables are taken as dimensions. A dimension table is created against each of the nominal variables and a foreign key is created to link the fact table and dimension table. For the example purposes, the schema is generated for cluster C1 which is same as in the previous section.

5.3.5.2 Compute Data Cube

Once the STAR schema is ready, the model computes a data cube on the schema by importing all data from the cluster to this schema. The resultant data cube contains data in aggregate form. For example purposes, data of cluster C1 is imported in the data warehouse. Some sample data from the data cube is showing in Table 9. The numeric columns present the data in Average aggregate measure.

Table 9. 5 records sample taken from data cube constructed on the schema

Work Class	Education	Relationship	Race	Sex	Country	Age	Edu Num.	Hours Per Week
Private	HS-grad	Own-child	White	Female	Laos	23	13	40
Local Gov.	12th	Unmarried	Black	Male	US	18	9	40
Private	HS-grad	Own-child	Black	Male	Jamaica	23	10	50
Local Gov.	12th	Unmarried	White	Male	US	32	10	40
Local-gov	HS-grad	Own-child	Black	Female	Jamaica	31	9	60

5.3.5.3 Apply Classification Algorithms

This step takes the data cube generated in the previous step as input and applies classification algorithms on it. The classification algorithms include Multi-Layer Perceptron, Linear Regression and Simple Linear Regression.

For the implementation of this step, the data cube generated in the previous step is taken as example and classification algorithms are applied. These algorithms predict Average *Age* with the help of *Work Class, Marital Status* and *Education*. The evaluation measures are calculated for each of the algorithm for evaluation in the next step.

5.3.5.4 Evaluate Using Advanced Measures

After the classification algorithms are applied, the evaluation is done using measures namely Correlation Coefficient (CC), Mean absolute error (MSE), and Root mean squared error (RMSE). For the example data, these measures are calculated against each algorithm in the previous step. The values retrieved through the process are shown in the Table 10. The table provides these measures against all algorithms used for the prediction of Average *Age*.

Table 10. Evaluation results of algorithms using 3-top ranked variables for prediction

Algorithm	CC	MAE	RMSE
Multilayer Perceptron	0.2564	0.0451	0.0390
Simple Linear Regression	0.5449	0.0795	0.0965
Linear Regression	0.6647	0.0838	0.1076

CC = Correlation Coefficient, MAE = Mean Absolute Error, RMSE = Root Mean Squared Error

5.3.5.5 Predict Using Selected Algorithm

The last step of this process allows the selection of an algorithm from previous step and proceeds to prediction of the unknown instances based on the selected algorithm. The selection is based upon the values of advanced measures used in the model including Correlation Coefficient (CC), Mean absolute error (MSE), and Root mean squared error (RMSE). For the example, the best suited algorithm is Linear Regression. The Correlation Coefficient confirms that the prediction pattern is better and error rates MAE and RMSE are also lesser than the other models.

5.4 SUMMARY

In this chapter, the proposed model has been implemented on the *Adult* dataset. The pattern extraction module has been explained by taking a cluster on second layer, and by extracting association rules from it with the methodology discussed above in detail. This component now only allows the extraction but doesn't involve the user in the process, allows automatic generation of schema at different levels, uses advanced measures of evaluation and provides a mean for the users to visualize the results. The pattern prediction component provides ability to select classification model that fits the data, with the help of a series of steps explained above. This component has the ability to apply multiple algorithms at once, and evaluate these based on advanced measures. The evaluation process also includes a visualization component to assist the user to select a particular algorithm for prediction purposes. The next chapter includes the experimental study on a much larger dataset called *Forest Cover Type* taken from UCI Machine Learning website.

REFERENCES

Asuncion, A., & Newman, D. (2007). *UCI machine learning repository.* Academic Press.

Rosario, G. E., Rundensteiner, E. A., Brown, D. C., Ward, M. O., & Huang, S. (2004). Mapping nominal values to numbers for effective visualization. *Information Visualization*, *3*(2), 80–95. doi:10.1057/palgrave.ivs.9500072

Usman, M., Pears, R., & Fong, A. C. M. (2013). Discovering diverse association rules from multidimensional schema. *Expert Systems with Applications*, *40*(15), 5975–5996. doi:10.1016/j.eswa.2013.05.031

Chapter 6
Experimental Study III:
Forest Cover Type Dataset

ABSTRACT

This chapter provides implementation of the proposed model on Forest Cover Type data set. The chapter includes the implementation of pattern extraction from this dataset by following a series of steps discussed in the proposed model chapter. It also includes detailed implementation of pattern prediction from Automobile dataset for prediction of numeric variables, nominal variables, and aggregate data. The implementation of pattern prediction is also a series of steps as discussed before.

6.1 DATASET INTRODUCTION

Forest Cover Type data set is taken from UCI Machine Learning website(Asuncion & Newman, 2007). The data set has a mixture of numerical and nominal type of variables (13 in total). The whole data set contains 5, 81,012 records. Ten variables of the dataset are numeric and rest three variables are nominal. Numeric variables include *Elevation, Aspect, Slope, Horizontal Distance To Hydrology, Vertical Distance To Hydrology, Horizontal Distance To Roadways, Hillshade 9am, Hillshade Noon, Hillshade 3pm, Horizontal Distance To Fire Points*. The nominal variables and their distinct values are shown in the Table 1.

DOI: 10.4018/978-1-5225-5029-7.ch006

Table 1. Nominal Variables along with their distinct values in the Forest Dataset

Nominal Variables	Distinct Values
Wilderness_Areas	Rawah_Wilderness_Area,Comanche_Peak_Wilderness_Area, Neota_Wilderness_Area. Cache_la_Poudre_Wilderness_Area
Soil_Type	SoilType, SoilType2, ..., SoilType40
Cover_Type	Spruce/Fir, Krummholz, Lodgepole_Pine, Aspen, Douglas-fir, Ponderosa_Pine, Cottonwood/Willow

6.2 PATTERN EXTRACTION

This section presents the first part of the proposed framework called Pattern Extraction. As discussed above, this part works through a series of steps where each step takes input from the previous step. The steps involve hierarchical clusters generation, ranking of variables, multi-dimensional scaling, schema generation, mining of association rules, advanced evaluation of association rules and visualization of extracted patterns. The sub sections below explain each step briefly and then provide implementation using the example dataset.

6.2.1 Generate Hierarchical Clusters

Since the data in this dataset has a very large side, the dataset is sampled before applying hierarchical clustering. Due to the fact that dataset had an unbalanced nature, Stratified random sampling is used in order to obtain an un-biased sample. All records were divided into subgroups in such way that representation of each class remained at same proportion in the sample. The sample size was 40,000 records selected randomly from the original data for clustering. Although the process adopted a stratified sampling method to produce a sample that retains the diversity of classes, the sample size was rather small at approximately 8% of the total volume of records. As a consequence, overall information loss could be high enough to prevent the accurate depiction of all trends and patterns which exist in the dataset.

After that, Hierarchical Clustering is applied as in other case studies on the sample generate dendogram. Afterwards, remaining data was distributed among all clusters by using Euclidean distance. Each cluster is labeled by giving simple abbreviations and shown these in the form of a tree as already done in the previous case study. For instance, the dataset is split into C1 and C2 at first level and in next level C1 is split into C11 and C12. These clusters are shown in a tree structure in Figure 1.

There are different variables involved in split of the clusters at each level. Moreover, each variable in every cluster will have a different variance than in the other cluster at same level. If all variables *Elevation, Aspect, Slope, Horizontal Distance To Hydrology, Vertical Distance To Hydrology, Horizontal Distance To Roadways, Hillshade 9am, Hillshade Noon, Hillshade 3pm, Horizontal Distance To Fire Points, Wilderness_Areas, Soil Type* and *Cover Type* were used to define the split of C1 into C11 and C12, then a variable having an impact on split will have greater variance in one of the child clusters and lesser in the other cluster. For example in our ranking step, we show that variables ranked top in cluster C11 do not retain their ranking position in the other cluster C12.

6.2.2 Rank Variables

After the dendrogram is created, the model applies Principal Component Analysis to rank the variables within each cluster. However since PCA only works on numeric data, the model applies another technique to convert nominal data into the numeric data to apply PCA. The model takes data of all nominal variables and converts it to numeric values using Rosarios's Approach (Rosario, Rundensteiner, Brown, Ward, & Huang, 2004). A detailed discussion on this approach has already been provided in the proposed model chapter.

6.2.2.1 Convert Nominal Variables to Numeric Variables

To convert nominal variables to numeric variables, input files for the cluster are prepared for the tool used for this method and conversion is performed.

Figure 1. Tree structure of hierarchical clusters

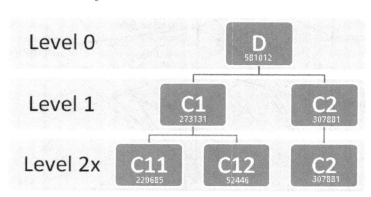

The quantified versions of selected variables in a Parallel Coordinates display are shown in Figure 2 for cluster C11. In parallel coordinates, each vertical line represents one variable, and each polyline cutting across the vertical axes represents instances in the dataset. The nominal variables *Wilderness Areas, Soil Type, Cover Type* are shown using vertical lines, where as distinct values with order and spacing are shown on the vertical lines. The variables are ordered such that the vertical axes of highly associated variables are positioned next to each other for easier interpretation. The semantic relationship is clear between nominal variables through polylines in the diagram. Once the process is completed, all data of the clusters is available in numeric format.

6.2.2.2 Apply Principal Component Analysis (PCA)

After the data is available in the numeric format, Principal Component Analysis is applied in order to measure the degree of variance for each variable and rank variables in the clusters. A detailed discussion on PCA has already been provided in proposed model chapter. Figure 3 shows the ranking of numeric variables in the three clusters after performing the PCA where as nominal variable ranking is shown in Figure 4. It is evident from Figures 3 and 4 that the list of nominal variables is unique across the clusters however the numerical variables list is not unique. The C1 and C11 clusters have the

Figure 2. Quantification display of Rossario's approach in parallel coordinates for cluster C11

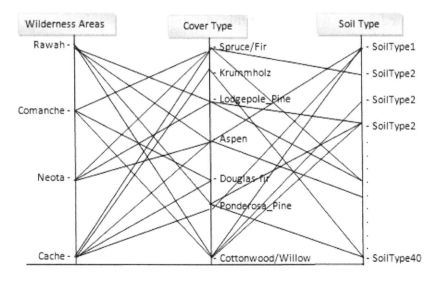

same number of variables, whereas C12 cluster has some variables which have zero variance and these are not used in the ranking process by SPSS.

6.2.3 Apply Multi-Dimensional Scaling

After the variables are ranked, the model defines natural grouping of all nominal variables involved in the prediction process. This process is called multi-dimensional scaling. A review of the grouping process is already provided in detail in proposed model chapter. Distinct values of all nominal variables are joined to form groups. The Figure 5 provides a view of variable groups in cluster C11 against different dimensions. For example, for *Cover Type* variable, the values *Spruce/Fir, Krummholz, Lodgepole_Pine, Aspen, Douglas-fir, Ponderosa_Pine* are kept in a single group showing the closeness with each other and therefore grouped together in a single group. The Group-Others is obtained by including all other values with no similarities with each other. Such grouping is hard to obtain in case of manual work. All nominal variable groups are obtained and input in a separate work sheet.

6.2.4 Generate STAR Schema

After grouping has been obtained, the model takes nominal variables as dimensions and numeric variables as facts to create a multidimensional STAR schema. A review of STAR schema has been given in proposed model chapter. This schema generation process is based on algorithms 1, 2

Figure 3. Ranking of numeric variables in forest dataset

C1		
Variable Name	**Calculated Value**	**Rank**
Hillshade_3pm	.86	1
Aspect	.71	2
Hillshade_Noon	.56	3
...	...	..
Horizontal_Distance_To_Fire_Points	-.29	10
Hillshade_9am	-.71	11

C11		
Variable Name	**Calculated Value**	**Rank**
Hillshade_3pm	.90	1
Elevation	.62	2
Slop	.43	3
...	...	..
Hillshade_9am	-.11	10
Horizontal_Distance_To_Fire_Points	-.65	11

C12		
Variable Name	**Calculated Value**	**Rank**
Horizontal_Distance_To_Hydrology	.74	1
Hillshade_Noon	.66	2
Aspect	.32	3
...	...	..
Elevation	-.20	10
Horizontal_Distance_To_Fire_Points	-1.88	1

Figure 4. Ranking of nominal variables in forest dataset

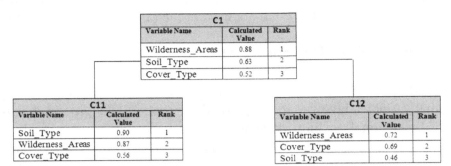

C1		
Variable Name	**Calculated Value**	**Rank**
Wilderness_Areas	0.88	1
Soil_Type	0.63	2
Cover_Type	0.52	3

C11		
Variable Name	**Calculated Value**	**Rank**
Soil_Type	0.90	1
Wilderness_Areas	0.87	2
Cover_Type	0.56	3

C12		
Variable Name	**Calculated Value**	**Rank**
Wilderness_Areas	0.72	1
Cover_Type	0.69	2
Soil_Type	0.46	3

as discussed in the same chapter. The multidimensional schema is created using top ranked variables. An example of multidimensional schema is given in Figure 5 which displays the schema for cluster C1. The schema contains a fact table with name CoverType_C1_Schema_Fact_Table. The top ranked dimensions were used to create three dimension tables: C1_dim_CoverType, C1_dim_Wilderness_Area and C1_dim_Soil_Type. The fact table contains all numeric columns as facts and all dimension names as foreign keys to the respective dimension tables.

Figure 5. Multidimensional schema of forest cover type dataset for cluster C1

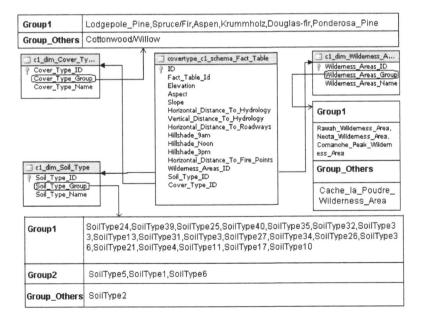

6.2.5 Mine Association Rules

After the schema is generated and data is in the data warehouse, the model extracts patterns in the form of association rules. A detailed discussion on association rule mining has already been provided in the proposed model chapter. Association rule mining is applied on original data as well as using the multidimensional schema for cluster C1. The results are shown in Table 2. This table shows the top 10 extracted patterns from cluster C1. These results are helpful for the analyst to get an abstract review of the cluster. Like in previous case study, the rules are compared with the approach of (Usman, Pears, & Fong, 2013). The rules generated from the approach in (Usman et al., 2013) are shown in the Table 3. It is clear that proposed approach provides better importance. It is evident that proposed approach provides more important rules than the approach in (Usman et al., 2013). Top ranked rule in previous approach has importance value 0.57 whereas proposed approach provides top ranked rule with important value of 0.95.

6.2.6 Evaluate Association Rules Using Advance Measures

Once the rules are obtained, these are evaluated using advanced measures. As described in the example data set in previous chapter that extracted patterns must be validated with advanced measures in order to measure the interestingness for the user, diversity measures called Rae, CON, and Hill

Table 2. Rule generated from our proposed methodology for cluster C1.

Rule	Imp.
1. Soil Type Grp = Group1,Wilderness Areas Grp = Group1→ CoverType = Krummholz	1.32
2.Soil Type Grp = Group 3 → Cover Type = Krummholz	1.29
3. Soil Type Grp = Group 1, Wilderness Areas Grp = Group 2 → Cover Type = Cottonwood/Willow	1.29
4. Soil Type Grp = Group 2, Wilderness Areas Grp = Group 2 → Cover Type = Ponderosa-Pine	1.28
5. Soil Type Grp = Group 4 →Cover Type = Krummholz	1.24
6. Soil Type Grp = Group-Others → Cover Type = Krummholz	1.23
7. Soil Type Grp = Group1, Wilderness Areas Grp = Group 3 →Cover Type = Ponderosa-Pine	1.21
9. Soil Typev = Group1, Wilderness Areas Grp = Group 4 → Cover Type = Spruce-fir	1.17
10. Soil Type Grp = Group 2 →Cover Type = Douglas-fir	1.05
11. Soil Type Grp = Group 4 → Cover Type = Krummholz	0.95

Table 3. Rules generated from the methodology proposed by (Usman et al., 2013)

Rule	Imp
1. Soil Type Grp = Group 3 → Cover Type = Krummholz	1.34
2. Soil Type Grp = Group1,Wilderness Areas Grp = Group1→ CoverType = Krummholz	1.30
3. Soil Type Grp = Group 1, Wilderness Areas Grp = Group 2 → Cover Type = Cottonwood/Willow	1.30
4. Soil Type Grp = Group 2, Wilderness Areas Grp = Group 2 → Cover Type = Ponderosa-Pine	1.29
5. Soil Type Grp = Group 4 →Cover Type = Krummholz	1.26
6. Soil Type Grp = Group-Others → Cover Type = Krummholz	1.24
7. Soil Type Grp = Group1, Wilderness Areas Grp = Group 3 →Cover Type = Ponderosa-Pine	1.23
8. Soil Type = Group1, Wilderness Areas Grp = Group 4 → Cover Type = Spruce-fir	1.19
9. Soil Type Grp = Group 2 →Cover Type = Douglas-fir	1.07
10. Soil Type Grp = Group 4 → Cover Type = Krummholz	0.98

measures are applied on extracted patterns. The process also calculates the same for non-schema rules. It is evident that the diversity values are greater for schema rules in all cases. The results are shown in Table 4. It is evident that there is an increase in diversity values in case generated schema is used. However since the data set contains only 3 nominal columns, select same columns are selected as in the proposed model of (Usman et al., 2013), so results of diversity are same in both cases.

6.2.7 Visualize Association Rules

The generated rules are visualized using a graphical interface in order to assist the analysts in the mining process as described in the previous experimental study.

6.3 PATTERN PREDICTION

This section presents the second module of the proposed framework called Pattern Prediction. As discussed in proposed model chapter, this module works through a series of steps where each step takes input from the previous step. The process starts by obtaining hierarchical clusters and ranking of variables. After ranking, Path P1, P2 and P3 are adapted to derive a classification model, which is evaluated in the next step. The selection of path depends upon the nature of variable being predicted. After evaluation, a model is selected to predict the patterns.

Table 4. Comparison of diversity measures between proposed model (rules with schema) and without schema rules

Clusters	Rule Set	Rae		CON		Hill	
		No Schema	With Schema	No Schema	With Schema	No Schema	With Schema
C1	R1-R6	0.230	0.278	0.277	0.366	-2.987	-2.293
	R1-R7	0.239	0.256	0.342	0.364	-2.646	-2.510
	R1-R8	0.226	0.240	0.34	0.363	-2.77	-2.712
	R1-R9	0.184	0.238	0.288	0.378	-3.764	-2.731
	R1-R10	0.176	0.234	0.292	0.386	-4.005	-2.780
C11	R1-R6	0.275	0.296	0.361	0.394	-2.338	-1.884
	R1-R7	0.247	0.281	0.351	0.402	-2.644	-1.999
	R1-R8	0.228	0.244	0.344	0.369	-2.892	-2.393
	R1-R9	0.187	0.229	0.292	0.364	-3.884	-2.573
	R1-R10	0.161	0.196	0.258	0.327	-4.81	-3.131
C12	R1-R6	0.219	0.284	0.251	0.376	-3.304	-2.294
	R1-R7	0.181	0.278	0.208	0.397	-4.273	-2.353
	R1-R8	0.163	0.263	0.209	0.397	-4.749	-2.509
	R1-R9	0.149	0.225	0.208	0.359	-5.195	-2.509
	R1-R10	0.137	0.205	0.203	0.342	-5.757	-3.348

6.3.1 Generate Hierarchical Clusters

The first step in pattern prediction involves hierarchical clusters generation like pattern extraction. The step creates clusters at different levels in the hierarchy for further mining purposes. The hierarchical clustering mechanism has already been discussed in detail in pattern extraction section of previous chapter. For pattern prediction, previous clustering results are used.

6.3.2 Rank Variables

Once the clusters are obtained, the ranking process is started to rank variables. In this component, a different process of ranking the available variables is adapted. This ranking process is based on normality of variables as discussed previously. Normality curves are drawn for each of the variable in each cluster and top ranked variables are picked. If a variable contains data which satisfies normality better than the other variables, it is considered to have more effect on classification. The ranking results are given in Figure 6.

Figure 6. Visualization of pattern extraction process of cluster C11

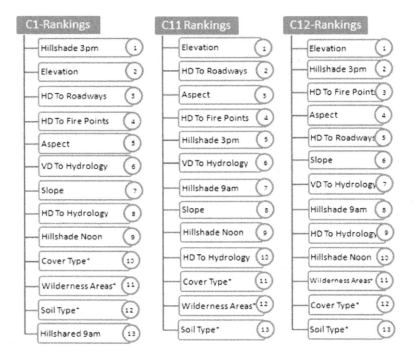

6.3.3 Prediction of Nominal Variable

If the variable to be predicted in a nominal variable the model adapts Path P1. This path is a series of steps. It takes ranking of variables as input along with the cluster data. In the first step classification algorithms are applied and results are gathered. These algorithms are evaluated using advanced measures in the next step to select a particular algorithm. In the last step actual prediction is done using the selected algorithm.

6.3.3.1 Apply Classification Algorithms

The model first generates association rules using Apriori Algorithm and calculates accuracy. The test is performed 10 times to get an average of accuracy. After that a set of classification algorithms is tested and results are calculated. The algorithms include Naïve Bayes, NN, VQNN, OWANN, J48, FuzzyNN, FONN and algorithms. The details of these algorithms are given in proposed model chapter.

For example purposes, cluster C11 is chosen. The model first generates association rules using Apriori Algorithm for the cluster, and calculates accuracy. The test is performed 10 times and an average of accuracy is calculated. Now, *Cover Type* is predicted by using top-ranked variables with the help of different classification algorithms. The prediction is done by creating an ARFF file for Weka Tool and 10-fold cross validation is used in the process. Advanced measures of evaluation like Accuracy, Time Consumption, Recall, Precision and F-Measure for each algorithm are also calculated. The time taken to build each classification model using top-ranked variables is also calculated. The classification models are run again by using all variables for prediction to draw a comparison. The results are passed to the next step for evaluation purposes.

6.3.3.2 Evaluate Using Advanced Measures

Once the results are ready, these results are passed to this step for advanced evaluation. This step allows the evaluation of algorithm based upon Accuracy, Recall, Precision and F-Measures. A review of these measures is provided in the proposed model chapter. This step also involves the visualization component which strengthens the process as well as enables the selection of an algorithm in better way. The visualization component allows the visualization of one algorithm at once. It involves a graphical display of Accuracy, Precision, Recall, and F-Measures along with the support to see the values in a tabular format. The table contains values for these measures along with the time taken in model building in milliseconds.

For cluster C11, the results calculated in the previous step are given in Table 5. Same results are shown in Figure 8 where an algorithm can be visualized for all the measures calculated in the table. The left hand side of the visualization component shows advanced measures called Recall, Precision and F-Measure which makes it easier for the analyst to review. The middle section of the visualization component shows the percentage of correctly and incorrectly classified instances based on the accuracy measure. The measures are shown in a tabular format on right side of the visualization component. Moreover, the time consumption in case of selected variables and all variables is also compared in the Table 6 and Figure 7. The results not only show that selection of variables has a big impact on time consumption. But it also allows the user to compare all algorithms based on time consumption at once.

Table 5. Evaluation results of algorithms using 3-top ranked variables for prediction C11

Algorithm	Accuracy	Time (s)	Recall	Precision	F-Measure
NN	65.36%	0	0.654	0.65	0.637
VQNN	65.36%	0.01	0.654	0.65	0.637
OWANN	64.98%	0	0.65	0.644	0.641
J 48	66.16%	0.29	0.662	0.694	0.616
FuzzyNN	09.83%	0.02	0.098	0.254	0.134
FONN	65.36%	0.01	0.654	0.65	0.637
Naïve Bayes	74.55%	0.1	0.651	0.649	0.649
Apriori	64.60%	-	-	-	-

Table 6. Time consumption (ms) different algorithms for forest cover type data set (C1 Cluster)

Variables Used	NN	VQNN	OWANN	J 48	FuzzyNN	FONN	Naïve Bayes
All Variables	500	460	600	7040	470	440	620
Selected Variables	150	140	170	2970	160	100	100

Figure 7. Comparison of time (ms) required to build the model using all variables and using top-ranked variables for cluster C1

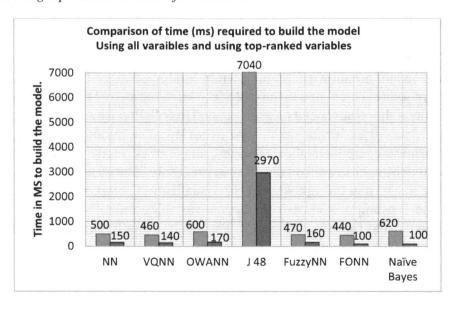

Figure 8. Visualization of Naïve Bayes classifier against advanced measures

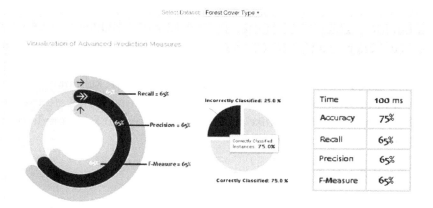

6.3.3.3 Predict Using Selected Algorithm

The last step of this process allows the selection of an algorithm from previous step and proceeds to prediction of the unknown instances based on the selected algorithm. The selection is based upon the values of advanced measures used in the model including Accuracy, Recall, Precision and F-Measure. The model also calculates Time for building the model which can also be considered for evaluation. For the example, the best suited algorithm is Naïve Bayes which provides highest values for all measures.

6.3.4 Prediction of Numeric Variable

Likewise, if the variable to be predicted in a numeric variable the model adapts Path P2. This path is also a series of steps. It takes ranking of variables as input along with the cluster data from the previous stage like prediction of nominal variable. In the first step the process creates a STAR schema and then applies classification algorithms to gather results. These algorithms are evaluated using advanced measures in the next step like before to select a particular algorithm. In the last step actual prediction is done using the selected algorithm.

6.3.4.1 Generate STAR Schema

The input for this step is the cluster and top ranked variables. These variables are used to generate a STAR schema which is exploited further for prediction purposes. The schema generation process is same as described in the pattern extraction module. For the example dataset, the STAR schema is generated as shown in Figure 9. For example purposes, all dimensions are used in the schema as this schema will also be used for aggregate facts prediction in a data warehouse environment.

6.3.4.2 Apply Classification Algorithms

This step takes the STAR schema generated in the previous step as input and applies classification algorithms on it. The classification algorithms include Multi-Layer Perceptron, Linear Regression and Simple Linear Regression since the predicted variable is numeric in this case. A review of these algorithms is already presented in previous section.

For the implementation of this step, the data for cluster C1 is passed to WEKA tool like before and classification algorithms are applied. The variable *Vertical Distance To Hydrology* is predicted using the top-ranked variables (*Hillshade 3pm, Elevation and Horizontal Distance To Roadways*). The evaluation measures are calculated for each of the algorithm for evaluation in the next step.

6.3.4.3 Evaluate Using Advanced Measures

After the classification algorithms are applied, the evaluation is done using measures namely Correlation Coefficient (CC), Mean absolute error (MSE), and Root mean squared error (RMSE). A review of these measures is presented in the previous section. For the example cluster, these measures are calculated against each algorithm in the previous step. The values retrieved through the process are shown in the Table 7. The table provides these measures against all algorithms used for the prediction of *Vertical Distance to Hydrology*.

6.3.4.4 Predict Using Selected Algorithm

The last step of this process allows the selection of an algorithm from previous step and proceeds to prediction of the unknown instances based on the selected

Figure 9. Multidimensional schema for cluster C1 to predict numeric variables

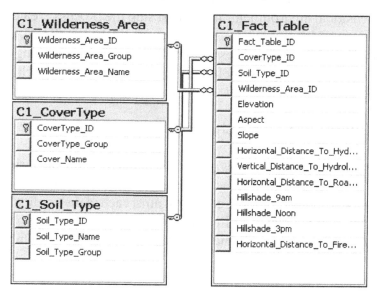

Table 7. Evaluation results of algorithms using 3-top ranked variables for prediction

Algorithm	CC	MAE	RMSE
Multilayer Perceptron	0.1385	0.0686	0.092
Simple Linear Regression	0.2205	0.0601	0.0839
Linear Regression	0.2277	0.06	0.0838

CC = Correlation Coefficient, MAE = Mean Absolute Error, RMSE = Root Mean Squared Error

algorithm. The selection is based upon the values of advanced measures used in the model including Correlation Coefficient (CC), Mean absolute error (MSE), and Root mean squared error (RMSE). For the example cluster, the best suited algorithm is Linear Regression. The Correlation Coefficient confirms that the prediction pattern is better and error rates MAE and RMSE are also lesser than the other models.

6.3.5 Prediction of Aggregate Data

The model also allows the prediction of aggregate data available in a multi-dimensional environment. In this case the model adapts Path P3. This path is also a series of steps. It takes ranking of variables as input along with the cluster data from the previous stage like prediction of aggregate data in the multi-dimensional environment. In the first step the process creates a STAR schema, generates data cube on top of the schema and then applies classification algorithms to gather results. These algorithms are evaluated using advanced measures in the next step like before to select a particular algorithm. In the last step actual prediction is done using the selected algorithm.

6.3.5.1 Generate STAR Schema

In this step, the process generates a STAR schema by using all variables. The numeric variables are taken as facts where as nominal variables are taken as dimensions. A dimension table is created against each of the nominal variables and a foreign key is created to link the fact table and dimension table. For the example purposes, the schema is generated for cluster C1 which is same as in the previous section.

One of the previous cases uses nominal variables to predict a nominal variable, where as the other enables to predict a numeric variable using top ranked numeric variables. There are cases where user is interested to predict aggregated numeric data or a dimension in data warehouse environment.

6.3.5.2 Compute Data Cube

Once the STAR schema is ready, the model computes a data cube on the schema by importing all data from the cluster to this schema. The resultant data cube contains data in aggregate form. For example purposes, data of cluster C1 is imported in the data warehouse. Some sample data from the data cube is showing in Table 8. The numeric columns present the data in Average aggregate measure.

6.3.5.3 Apply Classification Algorithms

This step takes the data cube generated in the previous step as input and applies classification algorithms on it. The classification algorithms include Multi-Layer Perceptron, Linear Regression and Simple Linear Regression.

For the implementation of this step, the data cube generated in the previous step is taken as example and classification algorithms are applied. These algorithms predict Average *Slope* with the help of *Elevation*, *Aspect*,

Table 8. 5 records sample taken from data cube constructed on the schema

Wilderness_Areas	Soil_Type	Cover_Type	Elevation	Aspect	Slope	Hillshade_9am	Hillshade_Noon
Rawah_Wilderness_Area	SoilType9	Krummholz	0.42	0.25	0.07	0.82	0.87
Neota_Wilderness_Area	SoilType18	Aspen	0.47	0.22	0.11	0.77	0.81
Rawah_Wilderness_Area	SoilType37	Krummholz	0.41	0.4	0.15	0.61	0.95
Neota_Wilderness_Area	SoilType18	Krummholz	0.40	0.89	0.11	0.74	0.84
Neota_Wilderness_Area	SoilType28	Aspen	0.43	0.84	0.11	0.78	0.96

Horizontal Distance to Hydrology variables. The evaluation measures are calculated for each of the algorithm for evaluation in the next step.

6.3.5.4 Evaluate Using Advanced Measures

After the classification algorithms are applied, the evaluation is done using measures namely Correlation Coefficient (CC), Mean absolute error (MSE), and Root mean squared error (RMSE). For the example data, these measures are calculated against each algorithm in the previous step. The values retrieved through the process are shown in the Table 9. The table provides these measures against all algorithms used for the prediction of Average *Slope.*

6.3.5.5 Predict Using Selected Algorithm

The last step of this process allows the selection of an algorithm from previous step and proceeds to prediction of the unknown instances based on the selected algorithm. The selection is based upon the values of advanced measures used in the model including Correlation Coefficient (CC), Mean absolute error

Table 9. Evaluation results of algorithms using 3-top ranked variables for prediction

Algorithms	CC	MAE	RMSE
Multilayer Perceptron	0.0256	0.083	0.1071
Simple Linear Regression	0.0562	0.0783	0.1001
Linear Regression	0.0873	0.0779	0.0999

CC = Correlation Coefficient, MAE = Mean Absolute Error, RMSE = Root Mean Squared Error

(MSE), and Root mean squared error (RMSE). For the example, the best suited algorithm is Linear Regression. The Correlation Coefficient confirms that the prediction pattern is better and error rates MAE and RMSE are also lesser than the other models.

6.4 SUMMARY

In this chapter, the proposed model has been explained with the help of *Forest Cover Type* data set. The pattern extraction module has been explained by taking a cluster on second layer, and by extracting association rules from it with the methodology discussed above in detail. This component now only allows the extraction but doesn't involve the user in the process, allows automatic generation of schema at different levels, uses advanced measures of evaluation and provides a mean for the users to visualize the results. The pattern prediction component provides ability to select classification model that fits the data, with the help of a series of steps explained above. This component has the ability to apply multiple algorithms at once, and evaluate these based on advanced measures. The evaluation process also includes a visualization component to assist the user to select a particular algorithm for prediction purposes.

REFERENCES

Asuncion, A., & Newman, D. (2007). *UCI machine learning repository.* Academic Press.

Rosario, G. E., Rundensteiner, E. A., Brown, D. C., Ward, M. O., & Huang, S. (2004). Mapping nominal values to numbers for effective visualization. *Information Visualization*, *3*(2), 80–95. doi:10.1057/palgrave.ivs.9500072

Usman, M., Pears, R., & Fong, A. C. M. (2013). Discovering diverse association rules from multidimensional schema. *Expert Systems with Applications*, *40*(15), 5975–5996. doi:10.1016/j.eswa.2013.05.031

Conclusion

This book has explored the usage of data mining and data warehousing techniques in hybrid fashion for pattern extraction and prediction in large data sets. The particular focus remained on creating domain knowledge independent technique which could work on multiple levels of abstraction, deploys advanced measures of evaluation on extract patterns and has the visualization capability for better understanding of patterns in a graphical interface. The experimental studies on three datasets have shown the potential of this methodology. In this concluding chapter, a summary of thesis presented and future guidelines are discussed.

This research work was motivated by the fact that there was no integrated framework available for pattern extraction and prediction in large datasets. Pattern extraction and prediction has been done previously separately. These techniques also have few issues which are addressed in the framework proposed in this research work.

Firstly, there are techniques which handle the issue of domain independency by only taking necessary dimensions for the mining process. This way, user is not involved in picking up the dimensions. Some of these techniques are able to reduce the dimensions, however, these results in removing some dimensions having interesting patterns. For instance, one of the techniques doesn't involve user in the feature selection process, but it ranks numeric and nominal data separately. The inter-relation between different types of data is not considered while ranking is done. The proposed framework ranks both types of data at once in ranking.

Secondly, in past pattern extraction and prediction over data warehouses has not been done at multiple levels in most cases. Usman, Pears, and Fong (2013) has adapted a multi-level approach to mine STAR schema which shows that it is worth mining at multiple levels for business analysts. The schema is generated at cluster level within levels of hierarchy. This process remains cumbersome while mining a large data set, since it has to work at each cluster level to create a schema for mining. Moreover, it takes a lot of time to manually copy the data from data source to the data warehouse manually. To handle these issues, the research work has presented two algorithms. One algorithm creates multi-dimensional schema at all levels for all clusters. The other algorithm shifts data from original dataset to the schema.

Thirdly, the evaluation of extracted and predicted patterns in these techniques is majorly achieved using conventional measures like Count, Support and Confidence, and Accuracy. These measures were designed to work with the transactional databases only. Researchers have proposed some advanced measures in particular for mining in a data warehouse environment. These measures are based on aggregate data, and thus are more meaningful that the conventional measures. The proposed framework provides the ability to evaluate the results using advanced measures like Rae, CON, Hill, F-Measure, ReCall, and Precision etc.

Finally, for visualization, it is perceptible that most techniques do not provide visualization whereas it is a helpful addition to the mining process. Some of the techniques however provide this support but at the same time, these are sensitive to large number of rules. Most of these techniques are although able to display the rules in small available space in the interface, but these are not interpretable. Authors have used Ball and Bar Graphs mostly, and it is not easy to distinguish between width and height of balls and bars respectively where researcher has a large resultant set of rules. The approaches which use shades of colors to distinguish rules are also troublesome. It is not easy to differentiate between same shades, as more shades will be used when more rules are generated. Another issue in these techniques is the inability to provide support for showing rules satisfying advanced measures, as most of these only focus support and confidence filters. To handle these issues, the proposed framework provides visualization components for pattern extraction and prediction. These components not only allow filters of advanced measures, but also handle large data sets effectively.

FUTURE WORK

The results presented in this thesis have shown the potential of this approach in pattern extraction and prediction in large datasets. However, due to limited time, some useful methods were not explored as detailed below.

Normality Measure

In pattern prediction, ranking is done using normality measure. The process orders the variables in a way that a variable satisfying the normal curve better than the other is given priority. The ranking process is done by creation of normal curves of variables and top ranked variables are picked for further mining process. Any statistical approach is not adapted due limited timescale which involves some statistical evidence for better normality value.

Multi-Dimensional Schema

Pattern extraction and prediction involves generation of a multi-dimensional schema on third stage. However, only STAR schema has been adapted in these cases. Other schemas like Snowflake and Fact Constellation are not targeted due to short time in MS thesis.

Visualization Component

The evaluation of classification models is supported by a visualization component. This visualization component allows the analyst to evaluate models one by one. However, for better selection and ease of the user, an interface displaying evaluation measures graphically in a single interface is highly desired. Due to lack of time, an interface with ability to show all models at once was not created. Such component, if created, will be helpful for time saving.

All-in-One Framework

Currently, all components in the framework are standalone components. The hierarchical clustering is supported by HCE Explorer, Ranking is done from SPSS or Weka Tool, Multi-dimensional Scaling and Schema generation is done using a .Net Application, Association Rule Mining is done using SQL Server, Advanced Evaluation of patterns is done using a .Net Application, and Visualization has been achieved using another component which is based on PHP and MYSQL. It is highly desired that an all-in-1 framework is developed to perform all tasks within it.

REFERENCES

Usman, M., Pears, R., & Fong, A. C. M. (2013). Discovering diverse association rules from multidimensional schema. *Expert Systems with Applications*, *40*(15), 5975–5996. doi:10.1016/j.eswa.2013.05.031

Related Readings

To continue IGI Global's long-standing tradition of advancing innovation through emerging research, please find below a compiled list of recommended IGI Global book chapters and journal articles in the areas of data storage, decentralized computing, and data mining. These related readings will provide additional information and guidance to further enrich your knowledge and assist you with your own research.

Abidi, N., Bandyopadhayay, A., & Gupta, V. (2017). Sustainable Supply Chain Management: A Three Dimensional Framework and Performance Metric for Indian IT Product Companies. *International Journal of Information Systems and Supply Chain Management*, *10*(1), 29–52. doi:10.4018/IJISSCM.2017010103

Achahbar, O., & Abid, M. R. (2015). The Impact of Virtualization on High Performance Computing Clustering in the Cloud. *International Journal of Distributed Systems and Technologies*, *6*(4), 65–81. doi:10.4018/IJDST.2015100104

Adhikari, M., Das, A., & Mukherjee, A. (2016). Utility Computing and Its Utilization. In G. Deka, G. Siddesh, K. Srinivasa, & L. Patnaik (Eds.), *Emerging Research Surrounding Power Consumption and Performance Issues in Utility Computing* (pp. 1–21). Hershey, PA: IGI Global. doi:10.4018/978-1-4666-8853-7.ch001

Aggarwal, S., & Nayak, A. (2016). Mobile Big Data: A New Frontier of Innovation. In J. Aguado, C. Feijóo, & I. Martínez (Eds.), *Emerging Perspectives on the Mobile Content Evolution* (pp. 138–158). Hershey, PA: IGI Global. doi:10.4018/978-1-4666-8838-4.ch008

Akherfi, K., Harroud, H., & Gerndt, M. (2016). A Mobile Cloud Middleware to Support Mobility and Cloud Interoperability. *International Journal of Adaptive, Resilient and Autonomic Systems*, 7(1), 41–58. doi:10.4018/IJARAS.2016010103

Al-Hamami, M. A. (2015). The Impact of Big Data on Security. In A. Al-Hamami & G. Waleed al-Saadoon (Eds.), *Handbook of Research on Threat Detection and Countermeasures in Network Security* (pp. 276–298). Hershey, PA: IGI Global. doi:10.4018/978-1-4666-6583-5.ch015

Al Jabri, H. A., Al-Badi, A. H., & Ali, O. (2017). Exploring the Usage of Big Data Analytical Tools in Telecommunication Industry in Oman. *Information Resources Management Journal*, 30(1), 1–14. doi:10.4018/IRMJ.2017010101

Alohali, B. (2016). Security in Cloud of Things (CoT). In Z. Ma (Ed.), *Managing Big Data in Cloud Computing Environments* (pp. 46–70). Hershey, PA: IGI Global. doi:10.4018/978-1-4666-9834-5.ch003

Alohali, B. (2017). Detection Protocol of Possible Crime Scenes Using Internet of Things (IoT). In M. Moore (Ed.), *Cybersecurity Breaches and Issues Surrounding Online Threat Protection* (pp. 175–196). Hershey, PA: IGI Global. doi:10.4018/978-1-5225-1941-6.ch008

AlZain, M. A., Li, A. S., Soh, B., & Pardede, E. (2015). Multi-Cloud Data Management using Shamir's Secret Sharing and Quantum Byzantine Agreement Schemes. *International Journal of Cloud Applications and Computing*, 5(3), 35–52. doi:10.4018/IJCAC.2015070103

Armstrong, S., & Yampolskiy, R. V. (2017). Security Solutions for Intelligent and Complex Systems. In M. Dawson, M. Eltayeb, & M. Omar (Eds.), *Security Solutions for Hyperconnectivity and the Internet of Things* (pp. 37–88). Hershey, PA: IGI Global. doi:10.4018/978-1-5225-0741-3.ch003

Attasena, V., Harbi, N., & Darmont, J. (2015). A Novel Multi-Secret Sharing Approach for Secure Data Warehousing and On-Line Analysis Processing in the Cloud. *International Journal of Data Warehousing and Mining*, 11(2), 22–43. doi:10.4018/ijdwm.2015040102

Awad, W. S., & Abdullah, H. M. (2014). Improving the Security of Storage Systems: Bahrain Case Study. *International Journal of Mobile Computing and Multimedia Communications*, 6(3), 75–105. doi:10.4018/IJMCMC.2014070104

Bagui, S., & Nguyen, L. T. (2015). Database Sharding: To Provide Fault Tolerance and Scalability of Big Data on the Cloud. *International Journal of Cloud Applications and Computing*, *5*(2), 36–52. doi:10.4018/IJCAC.2015040103

Barbierato, E., Gribaudo, M., & Iacono, M. (2016). Modeling and Evaluating the Effects of Big Data Storage Resource Allocation in Global Scale Cloud Architectures. *International Journal of Data Warehousing and Mining*, *12*(2), 1–20. doi:10.4018/IJDWM.2016040101

Barbosa, J. L., Barbosa, D. N., Rigo, S. J., Machado de Oliveira, J., & Junior, S. A. (2017). Collaborative Learning on Decentralized Ubiquitous Environments. In L. Tomei (Ed.), *Exploring the New Era of Technology-Infused Education* (pp. 141–157). Hershey, PA: IGI Global. doi:10.4018/978-1-5225-1709-2.ch009

Benmounah, Z., Meshoul, S., & Batouche, M. (2017). Scalable Differential Evolutionary Clustering Algorithm for Big Data Using Map-Reduce Paradigm. *International Journal of Applied Metaheuristic Computing*, *8*(1), 45–60. doi:10.4018/IJAMC.2017010103

Bhadoria, R. S. (2016). Performance of Enterprise Architecture in Utility Computing. In G. Deka, G. Siddesh, K. Srinivasa, & L. Patnaik (Eds.), *Emerging Research Surrounding Power Consumption and Performance Issues in Utility Computing* (pp. 44–68). Hershey, PA: IGI Global. doi:10.4018/978-1-4666-8853-7.ch003

Bhardwaj, A. (2017). Solutions for Securing End User Data over the Cloud Deployed Applications. In M. Moore (Ed.), *Cybersecurity Breaches and Issues Surrounding Online Threat Protection* (pp. 198–218). Hershey, PA: IGI Global. doi:10.4018/978-1-5225-1941-6.ch009

Bibi, S., Katsaros, D., & Bozanis, P. (2015). Cloud Computing Economics. In V. Díaz, J. Lovelle, & B. García-Bustelo (Eds.), *Handbook of Research on Innovations in Systems and Software Engineering* (pp. 125–149). Hershey, PA: IGI Global. doi:10.4018/978-1-4666-6359-6.ch005

Bihl, T. J., Young, W. A. II, & Weckman, G. R. (2016). Defining, Understanding, and Addressing Big Data. *International Journal of Business Analytics*, *3*(2), 1–32. doi:10.4018/IJBAN.2016040101

Bimonte, S., Sautot, L., Journaux, L., & Faivre, B. (2017). Multidimensional Model Design using Data Mining: A Rapid Prototyping Methodology. *International Journal of Data Warehousing and Mining, 13*(1), 1–35. doi:10.4018/IJDWM.2017010101

Bruno, G. (2017). A Dataflow-Oriented Modeling Approach to Business Processes. *International Journal of Human Capital and Information Technology Professionals, 8*(1), 51–65. doi:10.4018/IJHCITP.2017010104

Chande, S. V. (2014). Cloud Database Systems: NoSQL, NewSQL, and Hybrid. In P. Raj & G. Deka (Eds.), *Handbook of Research on Cloud Infrastructures for Big Data Analytics* (pp. 216–231). Hershey, PA: IGI Global. doi:10.4018/978-1-4666-5864-6.ch009

Copie, A., Manațe, B., Munteanu, V. I., & Fortiș, T. (2015). An Internet of Things Governance Architecture with Applications in Healthcare. In F. Xhafa, P. Moore, & G. Tadros (Eds.), *Advanced Technological Solutions for E-Health and Dementia Patient Monitoring* (pp. 322–344). Hershey, PA: IGI Global. doi:10.4018/978-1-4666-7481-3.ch013

Cordeschi, N., Shojafar, M., Amendola, D., & Baccarelli, E. (2015). Energy-Saving QoS Resource Management of Virtualized Networked Data Centers for Big Data Stream Computing. In S. Bagchi (Ed.), *Emerging Research in Cloud Distributed Computing Systems* (pp. 122–155). Hershey, PA: IGI Global. doi:10.4018/978-1-4666-8213-9.ch004

Costan, A. A., Iancu, B., Rasa, P. C., Radu, A., Peculea, A., & Dadarlat, V. T. (2017). Intercloud: Delivering Innovative Cloud Services. In I. Hosu & I. Iancu (Eds.), *Digital Entrepreneurship and Global Innovation* (pp. 59–78). Hershey, PA: IGI Global. doi:10.4018/978-1-5225-0953-0.ch004

Croatti, A., Ricci, A., & Viroli, M. (2017). Towards a Mobile Augmented Reality System for Emergency Management: The Case of SAFE. *International Journal of Distributed Systems and Technologies, 8*(1), 46–58. doi:10.4018/IJDST.2017010104

David-West, O. (2016). Information and Communications Technology (ICT) and the Supply Chain. In B. Christiansen (Ed.), *Handbook of Research on Global Supply Chain Management* (pp. 495–515). Hershey, PA: IGI Global. doi:10.4018/978-1-4666-9639-6.ch028

Dawson, M. (2017). Exploring Secure Computing for the Internet of Things, Internet of Everything, Web of Things, and Hyperconnectivity. In M. Dawson, M. Eltayeb, & M. Omar (Eds.), *Security Solutions for Hyperconnectivity and the Internet of Things* (pp. 1–12). Hershey, PA: IGI Global. doi:10.4018/978-1-5225-0741-3.ch001

Delgado, J. C. (2015). An Interoperability Framework for Enterprise Applications in Cloud Environments. In N. Rao (Ed.), *Enterprise Management Strategies in the Era of Cloud Computing* (pp. 26–59). Hershey, PA: IGI Global. doi:10.4018/978-1-4666-8339-6.ch002

Dhal, S. K., Verma, H., & Addya, S. K. (2017). Resource and Energy Efficient Virtual Machine Migration in Cloud Data Centers. In A. Turuk, B. Sahoo, & S. Addya (Eds.), *Resource Management and Efficiency in Cloud Computing Environments* (pp. 210–238). Hershey, PA: IGI Global. doi:10.4018/978-1-5225-1721-4.ch009

Duggirala, S. (2014). Big Data Architecture: Storage and Computation. In P. Raj & G. Deka (Eds.), *Handbook of Research on Cloud Infrastructures for Big Data Analytics* (pp. 129–156). Hershey, PA: IGI Global. doi:10.4018/978-1-4666-5864-6.ch006

Easton, J., & Parmar, R. (2017). Navigating Your Way to the Hybrid Cloud. In J. Chen, Y. Zhang, & R. Gottschalk (Eds.), *Handbook of Research on End-to-End Cloud Computing Architecture Design* (pp. 15–38). Hershey, PA: IGI Global. doi:10.4018/978-1-5225-0759-8.ch002

Elkabbany, G. F., & Rasslan, M. (2017). Security Issues in Distributed Computing System Models. In M. Dawson, M. Eltayeb, & M. Omar (Eds.), *Security Solutions for Hyperconnectivity and the Internet of Things* (pp. 211–259). Hershey, PA: IGI Global. doi:10.4018/978-1-5225-0741-3.ch009

Elkhodr, M., Shahrestani, S., & Cheung, H. (2016). Wireless Enabling Technologies for the Internet of Things. In Q. Hassan (Ed.), *Innovative Research and Applications in Next-Generation High Performance Computing* (pp. 368–396). Hershey, PA: IGI Global. doi:10.4018/978-1-5225-0287-6.ch015

Elkhodr, M., Shahrestani, S., & Cheung, H. (2017). Internet of Things Research Challenges. In M. Dawson, M. Eltayeb, & M. Omar (Eds.), *Security Solutions for Hyperconnectivity and the Internet of Things* (pp. 13–36). Hershey, PA: IGI Global. doi:10.4018/978-1-5225-0741-3.ch002

Erturk, E. (2017). Cloud Computing and Cybersecurity Issues Facing Local Enterprises. In M. Moore (Ed.), *Cybersecurity Breaches and Issues Surrounding Online Threat Protection* (pp. 219–247). Hershey, PA: IGI Global. doi:10.4018/978-1-5225-1941-6.ch010

Ferreira da Silva, R., Glatard, T., & Desprez, F. (2015). Self-Management of Operational Issues for Grid Computing: The Case of the Virtual Imaging Platform. In S. Bagchi (Ed.), *Emerging Research in Cloud Distributed Computing Systems* (pp. 187–221). Hershey, PA: IGI Global. doi:10.4018/978-1-4666-8213-9.ch006

Fu, S., He, L., Liao, X., Huang, C., Li, K., & Chang, C. (2015). Analyzing and Boosting the Data Availability in Decentralized Online Social Networks. *International Journal of Web Services Research*, *12*(2), 47–72. doi:10.4018/IJWSR.2015040103

Gao, F., & Zhao, Q. (2014). Big Data Based Logistics Data Mining Platform: Architecture and Implementation. *International Journal of Interdisciplinary Telecommunications and Networking*, *6*(4), 24–34. doi:10.4018/IJITN.2014100103

Gudivada, V. N., Nandigam, J., & Paris, J. (2015). Programming Paradigms in High Performance Computing. In R. Segall, J. Cook, & Q. Zhang (Eds.), *Research and Applications in Global Supercomputing* (pp. 303–330). Hershey, PA: IGI Global. doi:10.4018/978-1-4666-7461-5.ch013

Hagos, D. H. (2016). Software-Defined Networking for Scalable Cloud-based Services to Improve System Performance of Hadoop-based Big Data Applications. *International Journal of Grid and High Performance Computing*, *8*(2), 1–22. doi:10.4018/IJGHPC.2016040101

Hallappanavar, V. L., & Birje, M. N. (2017). Trust Management in Cloud Computing. In M. Dawson, M. Eltayeb, & M. Omar (Eds.), *Security Solutions for Hyperconnectivity and the Internet of Things* (pp. 151–183). Hershey, PA: IGI Global. doi:10.4018/978-1-5225-0741-3.ch007

Hameur Laine, A., & Brahimi, S. (2017). Background on Context-Aware Computing Systems. In C. Reis & M. Maximiano (Eds.), *Internet of Things and Advanced Application in Healthcare* (pp. 1–31). Hershey, PA: IGI Global. doi:10.4018/978-1-5225-1820-4.ch001

Hamidi, H. (2017). A Model for Impact of Organizational Project Benefits Management and its Impact on End User. *Journal of Organizational and End User Computing*, 29(1), 51–65. doi:10.4018/JOEUC.2017010104

Hamidine, H., & Mahmood, A. (2017). Cloud Computing Data Storage Security Based on Different Encryption Schemes. In J. Chen, Y. Zhang, & R. Gottschalk (Eds.), *Handbook of Research on End-to-End Cloud Computing Architecture Design* (pp. 189–221). Hershey, PA: IGI Global. doi:10.4018/978-1-5225-0759-8.ch009

Hamidine, H., & Mahmood, A. (2017). Cloud Computing Data Storage Security Based on Different Encryption Schemes. In J. Chen, Y. Zhang, & R. Gottschalk (Eds.), *Handbook of Research on End-to-End Cloud Computing Architecture Design* (pp. 189–221). Hershey, PA: IGI Global. doi:10.4018/978-1-5225-0759-8.ch009

Hao, Y., & Helo, P. (2015). Cloud Manufacturing towards Sustainable Management. In F. Soliman (Ed.), *Business Transformation and Sustainability through Cloud System Implementation* (pp. 121–139). Hershey, PA: IGI Global. doi:10.4018/978-1-4666-6445-6.ch009

Hasan, N., & Rahman, A. A. (2017). Ranking the Factors that Impact Customers Online Participation in Value Co-creation in Service Sector Using Analytic Hierarchy Process. *International Journal of Information Systems in the Service Sector*, 9(1), 37–53. doi:10.4018/IJISSS.2017010103

Hashemi, S., Monfaredi, K., & Hashemi, S. Y. (2015). Cloud Computing for Secure Services in E-Government Architecture. *Journal of Information Technology Research*, 8(1), 43–61. doi:10.4018/JITR.2015010104

Hayajneh, S. M. (2015). Cloud Computing SaaS Paradigm for Efficient Modelling of Solar Features and Activities. *International Journal of Cloud Applications and Computing*, 5(3), 20–34. doi:10.4018/IJCAC.2015070102

Huang, L. K. (2017). A Cultural Model of Online Banking Adoption: Long-Term Orientation Perspective. *Journal of Organizational and End User Computing*, 29(1), 1–22. doi:10.4018/JOEUC.2017010101

Jacob, G., & Annamalai, M. (2017). Secure Storage and Transmission of Healthcare Records. In V. Tiwari, B. Tiwari, R. Thakur, & S. Gupta (Eds.), *Pattern and Data Analysis in Healthcare Settings* (pp. 7–34). Hershey, PA: IGI Global. doi:10.4018/978-1-5225-0536-5.ch002

Jadon, K. S., Mudgal, P., & Bhadoria, R. S. (2016). Optimization and Management of Resource in Utility Computing. In G. Deka, G. Siddesh, K. Srinivasa, & L. Patnaik (Eds.), *Emerging Research Surrounding Power Consumption and Performance Issues in Utility Computing* (pp. 22–43). Hershey, PA: IGI Global. doi:10.4018/978-1-4666-8853-7.ch002

Jararweh, Y., Al-Sharqawi, O., Abdulla, N., Tawalbeh, L., & Alhammouri, M. (2014). High-Throughput Encryption for Cloud Computing Storage System. *International Journal of Cloud Applications and Computing*, 4(2), 1–14. doi:10.4018/ijcac.2014040101

Jha, M., Jha, S., & O'Brien, L. (2017). Social Media and Big Data: A Conceptual Foundation for Organizations. In R. Chugh (Ed.), *Harnessing Social Media as a Knowledge Management Tool* (pp. 315–332). Hershey, PA: IGI Global. doi:10.4018/978-1-5225-0495-5.ch015

Kantarci, B., & Mouftah, H. T. (2015). Sensing as a Service in Cloud-Centric Internet of Things Architecture. In T. Soyata (Ed.), *Enabling Real-Time Mobile Cloud Computing through Emerging Technologies* (pp. 83–115). Hershey, PA: IGI Global. doi:10.4018/978-1-4666-8662-5.ch003

Kasemsap, K. (2015). The Role of Cloud Computing Adoption in Global Business. In V. Chang, R. Walters, & G. Wills (Eds.), *Delivery and Adoption of Cloud Computing Services in Contemporary Organizations* (pp. 26–55). Hershey, PA: IGI Global. doi:10.4018/978-1-4666-8210-8.ch002

Kasemsap, K. (2015). The Role of Cloud Computing in Global Supply Chain. In N. Rao (Ed.), *Enterprise Management Strategies in the Era of Cloud Computing* (pp. 192–219). Hershey, PA: IGI Global. doi:10.4018/978-1-4666-8339-6.ch009

Kasemsap, K. (2017). Mastering Intelligent Decision Support Systems in Enterprise Information Management. In G. Sreedhar (Ed.), *Web Data Mining and the Development of Knowledge-Based Decision Support Systems* (pp. 35–56). Hershey, PA: IGI Global. doi:10.4018/978-1-5225-1877-8.ch004

Kaukalias, T., & Chatzimisios, P. (2015). Internet of Things (IoT). In M. Khosrow-Pour (Ed.), *Encyclopedia of Information Science and Technology* (3rd ed.; pp. 7623–7632). Hershey, PA: IGI Global. doi:10.4018/978-1-4666-5888-2.ch751

Kavoura, A., & Koziol, L. (2017). Polish Firms' Innovation Capability for Competitiveness via Information Technologies and Social Media Implementation. In A. Vlachvei, O. Notta, K. Karantininis, & N. Tsounis (Eds.), *Factors Affecting Firm Competitiveness and Performance in the Modern Business World* (pp. 191–222). Hershey, PA: IGI Global. doi:10.4018/978-1-5225-0843-4.ch007

Khan, I. U., Hameed, Z., & Khan, S. U. (2017). Understanding Online Banking Adoption in a Developing Country: UTAUT2 with Cultural Moderators. *Journal of Global Information Management*, *25*(1), 43–65. doi:10.4018/JGIM.2017010103

Kirci, P. (2017). Ubiquitous and Cloud Computing: Ubiquitous Computing. In A. Turuk, B. Sahoo, & S. Addya (Eds.), *Resource Management and Efficiency in Cloud Computing Environments* (pp. 1–32). Hershey, PA: IGI Global. doi:10.4018/978-1-5225-1721-4.ch001

Kofahi, I., & Alryalat, H. (2017). Enterprise Resource Planning (ERP) Implementation Approaches and the Performance of Procure-to-Pay Business Processes: (Field Study in Companies that Implement Oracle ERP in Jordan). *International Journal of Information Technology Project Management*, *8*(1), 55–71. doi:10.4018/IJITPM.2017010104

Koumaras, H., Damaskos, C., Diakoumakos, G., Kourtis, M., Xilouris, G., Gardikis, G., & Siakoulis, T. et al. (2015). Virtualization Evolution: From IT Infrastructure Abstraction of Cloud Computing to Virtualization of Network Functions. In G. Mastorakis, C. Mavromoustakis, & E. Pallis (Eds.), *Resource Management of Mobile Cloud Computing Networks and Environments* (pp. 279–306). Hershey, PA: IGI Global. doi:10.4018/978-1-4666-8225-2.ch010

Kuada, E. (2017). Security and Trust in Cloud Computing. In M. Dawson, M. Eltayeb, & M. Omar (Eds.), *Security Solutions for Hyperconnectivity and the Internet of Things* (pp. 184–210). Hershey, PA: IGI Global. doi:10.4018/978-1-5225-0741-3.ch008

Kumar, D., Sahoo, B., & Mandal, T. (2015). Heuristic Task Consolidation Techniques for Energy Efficient Cloud Computing. In N. Rao (Ed.), *Enterprise Management Strategies in the Era of Cloud Computing* (pp. 238–260). Hershey, PA: IGI Global. doi:10.4018/978-1-4666-8339-6.ch011

Lee, C. K., Cao, Y., & Ng, K. H. (2017). Big Data Analytics for Predictive Maintenance Strategies. In H. Chan, N. Subramanian, & M. Abdulrahman (Eds.), *Supply Chain Management in the Big Data Era* (pp. 50–74). Hershey, PA: IGI Global. doi:10.4018/978-1-5225-0956-1.ch004

Liao, W. (2016). Application of Hadoop in the Document Storage Management System for Telecommunication Enterprise. *International Journal of Interdisciplinary Telecommunications and Networking*, 8(2), 58–68. doi:10.4018/IJITN.2016040106

Liew, C. S., Ang, J. M., Goh, Y. T., Koh, W. K., Tan, S. Y., & Teh, R. Y. (2017). Factors Influencing Consumer Acceptance of Internet of Things Technology. In N. Suki (Ed.), *Handbook of Research on Leveraging Consumer Psychology for Effective Customer Engagement* (pp. 186–201). Hershey, PA: IGI Global. doi:10.4018/978-1-5225-0746-8.ch012

Lytras, M. D., Raghavan, V., & Damiani, E. (2017). Big Data and Data Analytics Research: From Metaphors to Value Space for Collective Wisdom in Human Decision Making and Smart Machines. *International Journal on Semantic Web and Information Systems*, 13(1), 1–10. doi:10.4018/IJSWIS.2017010101

Mabe, L. K., & Oladele, O. I. (2017). Application of Information Communication Technologies for Agricultural Development through Extension Services: A Review. In T. Tossy (Ed.), *Information Technology Integration for Socio-Economic Development* (pp. 52–101). Hershey, PA: IGI Global. doi:10.4018/978-1-5225-0539-6.ch003

Machaka, P., & Nelwamondo, F. (2016). Data Mining Techniques for Distributed Denial of Service Attacks Detection in the Internet of Things: A Research Survey. In O. Isafiade & A. Bagula (Eds.), *Data Mining Trends and Applications in Criminal Science and Investigations* (pp. 275–334). Hershey, PA: IGI Global. doi:10.4018/978-1-5225-0463-4.ch010

Manohari, P. K., & Ray, N. K. (2017). A Comprehensive Study of Security in Cloud Computing. In N. Ray & A. Turuk (Eds.), *Handbook of Research on Advanced Wireless Sensor Network Applications, Protocols, and Architectures* (pp. 386–412). Hershey, PA: IGI Global. doi:10.4018/978-1-5225-0486-3.ch016

Manvi, S. S., & Hegde, N. (2017). Vehicular Cloud Computing Challenges and Security. In S. Bhattacharyya, N. Das, D. Bhattacharjee, & A. Mukherjee (Eds.), *Handbook of Research on Recent Developments in Intelligent Communication Application* (pp. 344–365). Hershey, PA: IGI Global. doi:10.4018/978-1-5225-1785-6.ch013

McKelvey, N., Curran, K., & Subaginy, N. (2015). The Internet of Things. In M. Khosrow-Pour (Ed.), *Encyclopedia of Information Science and Technology* (3rd ed.; pp. 5777–5783). Hershey, PA: IGI Global. doi:10.4018/978-1-4666-5888-2.ch570

Meddah, I. H., Belkadi, K., & Boudia, M. A. (2017). Efficient Implementation of Hadoop MapReduce based Business Process Dataflow. *International Journal of Decision Support System Technology*, *9*(1), 49–60. doi:10.4018/IJDSST.2017010104

Meghanathan, N. (2015). Virtualization as the Catalyst for Cloud Computing. In M. Khosrow-Pour (Ed.), *Encyclopedia of Information Science and Technology* (3rd ed.; pp. 1096–1110). Hershey, PA: IGI Global. doi:10.4018/978-1-4666-5888-2.ch105

Mehenni, T. (2017). Geographic Knowledge Discovery in Multiple Spatial Databases. In S. Faiz & K. Mahmoudi (Eds.), *Handbook of Research on Geographic Information Systems Applications and Advancements* (pp. 344–366). Hershey, PA: IGI Global. doi:10.4018/978-1-5225-0937-0.ch013

Mehrotra, S., & Kohli, S. (2017). Data Clustering and Various Clustering Approaches. In S. Bhattacharyya, S. De, I. Pan, & P. Dutta (Eds.), *Intelligent Multidimensional Data Clustering and Analysis* (pp. 90–108). Hershey, PA: IGI Global. doi:10.4018/978-1-5225-1776-4.ch004

Meralto, C., Moura, J., & Marinheiro, R. (2017). Wireless Mesh Sensor Networks with Mobile Devices: A Comprehensive Review. In N. Ray & A. Turuk (Eds.), *Handbook of Research on Advanced Wireless Sensor Network Applications, Protocols, and Architectures* (pp. 129–155). Hershey, PA: IGI Global. doi:10.4018/978-1-5225-0486-3.ch005

Moradbeikie, A., Abrishami, S., & Abbasi, H. (2016). Creating Time-Limited Attributes for Time-Limited Services in Cloud Computing. *International Journal of Information Security and Privacy*, *10*(4), 44–57. doi:10.4018/IJISP.2016100103

Mourtzoukos, K., Kefalakis, N., & Soldatos, J. (2015). Open Source Object Directory Services for Inter-Enterprise Tracking and Tracing Applications. In I. Lee (Ed.), *RFID Technology Integration for Business Performance Improvement* (pp. 80–97). Hershey, PA: IGI Global. doi:10.4018/978-1-4666-6308-4.ch004

Mugisha, E., Zhang, G., El Abidine, M. Z., & Eugene, M. (2017). A TPM-based Secure Multi-Cloud Storage Architecture grounded on Erasure Codes. *International Journal of Information Security and Privacy*, *11*(1), 52–64. doi:10.4018/IJISP.2017010104

Munir, K. (2017). Security Model for Mobile Cloud Database as a Service (DBaaS). In K. Munir (Ed.), *Security Management in Mobile Cloud Computing* (pp. 169–180). Hershey, PA: IGI Global. doi:10.4018/978-1-5225-0602-7.ch008

Murugaiyan, S. R., Chandramohan, D., Vengattaraman, T., & Dhavachelvan, P. (2014). A Generic Privacy Breach Preventing Methodology for Cloud Based Web Service. *International Journal of Grid and High Performance Computing*, *6*(3), 53–84. doi:10.4018/ijghpc.2014070104

Naeem, M. A., & Jamil, N. (2015). Online Processing of End-User Data in Real-Time Data Warehousing. In M. Usman (Ed.), *Improving Knowledge Discovery through the Integration of Data Mining Techniques* (pp. 13–31). Hershey, PA: IGI Global. doi:10.4018/978-1-4666-8513-0.ch002

Nayak, P. (2017). Internet of Things Services, Applications, Issues, and Challenges. In N. Ray & A. Turuk (Eds.), *Handbook of Research on Advanced Wireless Sensor Network Applications, Protocols, and Architectures* (pp. 353–368). Hershey, PA: IGI Global. doi:10.4018/978-1-5225-0486-3.ch014

Nekaj, E. L. (2017). The Crowd Economy: From the Crowd to Businesses to Public Administrations and Multinational Companies. In W. Vassallo (Ed.), *Crowdfunding for Sustainable Entrepreneurship and Innovation* (pp. 1–19). Hershey, PA: IGI Global. doi:10.4018/978-1-5225-0568-6.ch001

Omar, M. (2015). Cloud Computing Security: Abuse and Nefarious Use of Cloud Computing. In K. Munir, M. Al-Mutairi, & L. Mohammed (Eds.), *Handbook of Research on Security Considerations in Cloud Computing* (pp. 30–38). Hershey, PA: IGI Global. doi:10.4018/978-1-4666-8387-7.ch002

Orike, S., & Brown, D. (2016). Big Data Management: An Investigation into Wireless and Cloud Computing. *International Journal of Interdisciplinary Telecommunications and Networking*, 8(4), 34–50. doi:10.4018/IJITN.2016100104

Ouf, S., & Nasr, M. (2015). Cloud Computing: The Future of Big Data Management. *International Journal of Cloud Applications and Computing*, 5(2), 53–61. doi:10.4018/IJCAC.2015040104

Ozpinar, A., & Yarkan, S. (2016). Vehicle to Cloud: Big Data for Environmental Sustainability, Energy, and Traffic Management. In M. Singh, & D. G. (Eds.), Effective Big Data Management and Opportunities for Implementation (pp. 182-201). Hershey, PA: IGI Global. doi:10.4018/978-1-5225-0182-4.ch012

Pal, A., & Kumar, M. (2017). Collaborative Filtering Based Data Mining for Large Data. In V. Bhatnagar (Ed.), *Collaborative Filtering Using Data Mining and Analysis* (pp. 115–127). Hershey, PA: IGI Global. doi:10.4018/978-1-5225-0489-4.ch006

Pal, K., & Karakostas, B. (2016). A Game-Based Approach for Simulation and Design of Supply Chains. In T. Kramberger, V. Potočan, & V. Ipavec (Eds.), *Sustainable Logistics and Strategic Transportation Planning* (pp. 1–23). Hershey, PA: IGI Global. doi:10.4018/978-1-5225-0001-8.ch001

Panda, S. (2017). Security Issues and Challenges in Internet of Things. In N. Ray & A. Turuk (Eds.), *Handbook of Research on Advanced Wireless Sensor Network Applications, Protocols, and Architectures* (pp. 369–385). Hershey, PA: IGI Global. doi:10.4018/978-1-5225-0486-3.ch015

Pandit, S., Milman, I., Oberhofer, M., & Zhou, Y. (2017). Principled Reference Data Management for Big Data and Business Intelligence. *International Journal of Organizational and Collective Intelligence*, 7(1), 47–66. doi:10.4018/IJOCI.2017010104

Paul, A. K., & Sahoo, B. (2017). Dynamic Virtual Machine Placement in Cloud Computing. In A. Turuk, B. Sahoo, & S. Addya (Eds.), *Resource Management and Efficiency in Cloud Computing Environments* (pp. 136–167). Hershey, PA: IGI Global. doi:10.4018/978-1-5225-1721-4.ch006

Petri, I., Diaz-Montes, J., Zou, M., Zamani, A. R., Beach, T. H., Rana, O. F., & Rezgui, Y. et al. (2016). Distributed Multi-Cloud Based Building Data Analytics. In G. Kecskemeti, A. Kertesz, & Z. Nemeth (Eds.), *Developing Interoperable and Federated Cloud Architecture* (pp. 143–169). Hershey, PA: IGI Global. doi:10.4018/978-1-5225-0153-4.ch006

Poleto, T., Heuer de Carvalho, V. D., & Costa, A. P. (2017). The Full Knowledge of Big Data in the Integration of Inter-Organizational Information: An Approach Focused on Decision Making. *International Journal of Decision Support System Technology*, *9*(1), 16–31. doi:10.4018/IJDSST.2017010102

Rahman, N., & Iverson, S. (2015). Big Data Business Intelligence in Bank Risk Analysis. *International Journal of Business Intelligence Research*, *6*(2), 55–77. doi:10.4018/IJBIR.2015070104

Raj, P. (2014). Big Data Analytics Demystified. In P. Raj & G. Deka (Eds.), *Handbook of Research on Cloud Infrastructures for Big Data Analytics* (pp. 38–73). Hershey, PA: IGI Global. doi:10.4018/978-1-4666-5864-6.ch003

Raj, P. (2014). The Compute Infrastructures for Big Data Analytics. In P. Raj & G. Deka (Eds.), *Handbook of Research on Cloud Infrastructures for Big Data Analytics* (pp. 74–109). Hershey, PA: IGI Global. doi:10.4018/978-1-4666-5864-6.ch004

Raj, P. (2014). The Network Infrastructures for Big Data Analytics. In P. Raj & G. Deka (Eds.), *Handbook of Research on Cloud Infrastructures for Big Data Analytics* (pp. 157–185). Hershey, PA: IGI Global. doi:10.4018/978-1-4666-5864-6.ch007

Raman, A. C. (2014). Storage Infrastructure for Big Data and Cloud. In P. Raj & G. Deka (Eds.), *Handbook of Research on Cloud Infrastructures for Big Data Analytics* (pp. 110–128). Hershey, PA: IGI Global. doi:10.4018/978-1-4666-5864-6.ch005

Rao, A. P. (2017). Discovering Knowledge Hidden in Big Data from Machine-Learning Techniques. In G. Sreedhar (Ed.), *Web Data Mining and the Development of Knowledge-Based Decision Support Systems* (pp. 167–183). Hershey, PA: IGI Global. doi:10.4018/978-1-5225-1877-8.ch010

Rathore, M. M., Paul, A., Ahmad, A., & Jeon, G. (2017). IoT-Based Big Data: From Smart City towards Next Generation Super City Planning. *International Journal on Semantic Web and Information Systems*, *13*(1), 28–47. doi:10.4018/IJSWIS.2017010103

Ratten, V. (2015). An Entrepreneurial Approach to Cloud Computing Design and Application: Technological Innovation and Information System Usage. In S. Aljawarneh (Ed.), *Advanced Research on Cloud Computing Design and Applications* (pp. 1–14). Hershey, PA: IGI Global. doi:10.4018/978-1-4666-8676-2.ch001

Rebekah, R. D., Cheelu, D., & Babu, M. R. (2017). Necessity of Key Aggregation Cryptosystem for Data Sharing in Cloud Computing. In P. Krishna (Ed.), *Emerging Technologies and Applications for Cloud-Based Gaming* (pp. 210–227). Hershey, PA: IGI Global. doi:10.4018/978-1-5225-0546-4.ch010

Rehman, A., Ullah, R., & Abdullah, F. (2015). Big Data Analysis in IoT. In N. Zaman, M. Seliaman, M. Hassan, & F. Marquez (Eds.), *Handbook of Research on Trends and Future Directions in Big Data and Web Intelligence* (pp. 313–327). Hershey, PA: IGI Global. doi:10.4018/978-1-4666-8505-5.ch015

Rehman, M. H., Khan, A. U., & Batool, A. (2016). Big Data Analytics in Mobile and Cloud Computing Environments. In Q. Hassan (Ed.), *Innovative Research and Applications in Next-Generation High Performance Computing* (pp. 349–367). Hershey, PA: IGI Global. doi:10.4018/978-1-5225-0287-6.ch014

Rosado da Cruz, A. M., & Paiva, S. (2016). Cloud and Mobile: A Future Together. In A. Rosado da Cruz & S. Paiva (Eds.), *Modern Software Engineering Methodologies for Mobile and Cloud Environments* (pp. 1–20). Hershey, PA: IGI Global. doi:10.4018/978-1-4666-9916-8.ch001

Rusko, R. (2017). Strategic Turning Points in ICT Business: The Business Development, Transformation, and Evolution in the Case of Nokia. In I. Oncioiu (Ed.), *Driving Innovation and Business Success in the Digital Economy* (pp. 1–15). Hershey, PA: IGI Global. doi:10.4018/978-1-5225-1779-5.ch001

Sahlin, J. P. (2015). Federal Government Application of the Cloud Computing Application Integration Model. In M. Khosrow-Pour (Ed.), *Encyclopedia of Information Science and Technology* (3rd ed., pp. 2735–2744). Hershey, PA: IGI Global. doi:10.4018/978-1-4666-5888-2.ch267

Sahoo, S., Sahoo, B., Turuk, A. K., & Mishra, S. K. (2017). Real Time Task Execution in Cloud Using MapReduce Framework. In A. Turuk, B. Sahoo, & S. Addya (Eds.), *Resource Management and Efficiency in Cloud Computing Environments* (pp. 190–209). Hershey, PA: IGI Global. doi:10.4018/978-1-5225-1721-4.ch008

Schnjakin, M., & Meinel, C. (2014). Solving Security and Availability Challenges in Public Clouds. In A. Kayem & C. Meinel (Eds.), *Information Security in Diverse Computing Environments* (pp. 280–302). Hershey, PA: IGI Global. doi:10.4018/978-1-4666-6158-5.ch015

Shaikh, F. (2017). The Benefits of New Online (Digital) Technologies on Business: Understanding the Impact of Digital on Different Aspects of the Business. In I. Hosu & I. Iancu (Eds.), *Digital Entrepreneurship and Global Innovation* (pp. 1–17). Hershey, PA: IGI Global. doi:10.4018/978-1-5225-0953-0.ch001

Shalan, M. (2017). Cloud Service Footprint (CSF): Utilizing Risk and Governance Directions to Characterize a Cloud Service. In A. Turuk, B. Sahoo, & S. Addya (Eds.), *Resource Management and Efficiency in Cloud Computing Environments* (pp. 61–88). Hershey, PA: IGI Global. doi:10.4018/978-1-5225-1721-4.ch003

Sharma, A., & Tandekar, P. (2017). Cyber Security and Business Growth. In Rajagopal, & R. Behl (Eds.), Business Analytics and Cyber Security Management in Organizations (pp. 14-27). Hershey, PA: IGI Global. doi:10.4018/978-1-5225-0902-8.ch002

Shen, Y., Li, Y., Wu, L., Liu, S., & Wen, Q. (2014). Big Data Techniques, Tools, and Applications. In Y. Shen, Y. Li, L. Wu, S. Liu, & Q. Wen (Eds.), *Enabling the New Era of Cloud Computing: Data Security, Transfer, and Management* (pp. 185–212). Hershey, PA: IGI Global. doi:10.4018/978-1-4666-4801-2.ch009

Shen, Y., Li, Y., Wu, L., Liu, S., & Wen, Q. (2014). Cloud Infrastructure: Virtualization. In Y. Shen, Y. Li, L. Wu, S. Liu, & Q. Wen (Eds.), *Enabling the New Era of Cloud Computing: Data Security, Transfer, and Management* (pp. 51–76). Hershey, PA: IGI Global. doi:10.4018/978-1-4666-4801-2.ch003

Siddesh, G. M., Srinivasa, K. G., & Tejaswini, L. (2015). Recent Trends in Cloud Computing Security Issues and Their Mitigation. In G. Deka & S. Bakshi (Eds.), *Handbook of Research on Securing Cloud-Based Databases with Biometric Applications* (pp. 16–46). Hershey, PA: IGI Global. doi:10.4018/978-1-4666-6559-0.ch002

Singh, B., & K.S., J. (2017). Security Management in Mobile Cloud Computing: Security and Privacy Issues and Solutions in Mobile Cloud Computing. In K. Munir (Ed.), *Security Management in Mobile Cloud Computing* (pp. 148-168). Hershey, PA: IGI Global. doi:10.4018/978-1-5225-0602-7.ch007

Singh, J., Gimekar, A. M., & Venkatesan, S. (2017). An Overview of Big Data Security with Hadoop Framework. In M. Kumar (Ed.), *Applied Big Data Analytics in Operations Management* (pp. 165–181). Hershey, PA: IGI Global. doi:10.4018/978-1-5225-0886-1.ch008

Singh, S., & Singh, J. (2017). Management of SME's Semi Structured Data Using Semantic Technique. In M. Kumar (Ed.), *Applied Big Data Analytics in Operations Management* (pp. 133–164). Hershey, PA: IGI Global. doi:10.4018/978-1-5225-0886-1.ch007

Sokolowski, L., & Oussena, S. (2016). Using Big Data in Collaborative Learning. In M. Atzmueller, S. Oussena, & T. Roth-Berghofer (Eds.), *Enterprise Big Data Engineering, Analytics, and Management* (pp. 221–237). Hershey, PA: IGI Global. doi:10.4018/978-1-5225-0293-7.ch013

Soliman, F. (2015). Evaluation of Cloud System Success Factors in Supply-Demand Chains. In F. Soliman (Ed.), *Business Transformation and Sustainability through Cloud System Implementation* (pp. 90–104). Hershey, PA: IGI Global. doi:10.4018/978-1-4666-6445-6.ch007

Srinivasan, S. (2014). Meeting Compliance Requirements while using Cloud Services. In S. Srinivasan (Ed.), *Security, Trust, and Regulatory Aspects of Cloud Computing in Business Environments* (pp. 127–144). Hershey, PA: IGI Global. doi:10.4018/978-1-4666-5788-5.ch007

Sun, X., & Wei, Z. (2015). The Dynamic Data Privacy Protection Strategy Based on the CAP Theory. *International Journal of Interdisciplinary Telecommunications and Networking*, 7(1), 44–56. doi:10.4018/ijitn.2015010104

Sundararajan, S., Bhasi, M., & Pramod, K. (2017). Managing Software Risks in Maintenance Projects, from a Vendor Perspective: A Case Study in Global Software Development. *International Journal of Information Technology Project Management, 8*(1), 35–54. doi:10.4018/IJITPM.2017010103

Sundaresan, M., & Boopathy, D. (2014). Different Perspectives of Cloud Security. In S. Srinivasan (Ed.), *Security, Trust, and Regulatory Aspects of Cloud Computing in Business Environments* (pp. 73–90). Hershey, PA: IGI Global. doi:10.4018/978-1-4666-5788-5.ch004

Sutagundar, A. V., & Hatti, D. (2017). Data Management in Internet of Things. In N. Kamila (Ed.), *Handbook of Research on Wireless Sensor Network Trends, Technologies, and Applications* (pp. 80–97). Hershey, PA: IGI Global. doi:10.4018/978-1-5225-0501-3.ch004

Swacha, J. (2014). Measuring and Managing the Economics of Information Storage. In T. Tsiakis, T. Kargidis, & P. Katsaros (Eds.), *Approaches and Processes for Managing the Economics of Information Systems* (pp. 47–65). Hershey, PA: IGI Global. doi:10.4018/978-1-4666-4983-5.ch003

Swarnkar, M., & Bhadoria, R. S. (2016). Security Aspects in Utility Computing. In G. Deka, G. Siddesh, K. Srinivasa, & L. Patnaik (Eds.), *Emerging Research Surrounding Power Consumption and Performance Issues in Utility Computing* (pp. 262–275). Hershey, PA: IGI Global. doi:10.4018/978-1-4666-8853-7.ch012

Talamantes-Padilla, C. A., García-Alcaráz, J. L., Maldonado-Macías, A. A., Alor-Hernández, G., Sánchéz-Ramírez, C., & Hernández-Arellano, J. L. (2017). Information and Communication Technology Impact on Supply Chain Integration, Flexibility, and Performance. In M. Tavana, K. Szabat, & K. Puranam (Eds.), *Organizational Productivity and Performance Measurements Using Predictive Modeling and Analytics* (pp. 213–234). Hershey, PA: IGI Global. doi:10.4018/978-1-5225-0654-6.ch011

Tang, Z., & Pan, Y. (2015). Big Data Security Management. In N. Zaman, M. Seliaman, M. Hassan, & F. Marquez (Eds.), *Handbook of Research on Trends and Future Directions in Big Data and Web Intelligence* (pp. 53–66). Hershey, PA: IGI Global. doi:10.4018/978-1-4666-8505-5.ch003

Thakur, P. K., & Verma, A. (2015). Process Batch Offloading Method for Mobile-Cloud Computing Platform. *Journal of Cases on Information Technology*, *17*(3), 1–13. doi:10.4018/JCIT.2015070101

Thota, C., Manogaran, G., Lopez, D., & Vijayakumar, V. (2017). Big Data Security Framework for Distributed Cloud Data Centers. In M. Moore (Ed.), *Cybersecurity Breaches and Issues Surrounding Online Threat Protection* (pp. 288–310). Hershey, PA: IGI Global. doi:10.4018/978-1-5225-1941-6.ch012

Toor, G. S., & Ma, M. (2017). Security Issues of Communication Networks in Smart Grid. In M. Ferrag & A. Ahmim (Eds.), *Security Solutions and Applied Cryptography in Smart Grid Communications* (pp. 29–49). Hershey, PA: IGI Global. doi:10.4018/978-1-5225-1829-7.ch002

Wahi, A. K., Medury, Y., & Misra, R. K. (2015). Big Data: Enabler or Challenge for Enterprise 2.0. *International Journal of Service Science, Management, Engineering, and Technology*, *6*(2), 1–17. doi:10.4018/ijssmet.2015040101

Wang, H., Liu, W., & Soyata, T. (2014). Accessing Big Data in the Cloud Using Mobile Devices. In P. Raj & G. Deka (Eds.), *Handbook of Research on Cloud Infrastructures for Big Data Analytics* (pp. 444–470). Hershey, PA: IGI Global. doi:10.4018/978-1-4666-5864-6.ch018

Wang, M., & Kerr, D. (2017). Confidential Data Storage Systems for Wearable Platforms. In A. Marrington, D. Kerr, & J. Gammack (Eds.), *Managing Security Issues and the Hidden Dangers of Wearable Technologies* (pp. 74–97). Hershey, PA: IGI Global. doi:10.4018/978-1-5225-1016-1.ch004

Winter, J. S. (2015). Privacy Challenges for the Internet of Things. In M. Khosrow-Pour (Ed.), *Encyclopedia of Information Science and Technology* (3rd ed.; pp. 4373–4383). Hershey, PA: IGI Global. doi:10.4018/978-1-4666-5888-2.ch429

Wolfe, M. (2017). Establishing Governance for Hybrid Cloud and the Internet of Things. In J. Chen, Y. Zhang, & R. Gottschalk (Eds.), *Handbook of Research on End-to-End Cloud Computing Architecture Design* (pp. 300–325). Hershey, PA: IGI Global. doi:10.4018/978-1-5225-0759-8.ch013

Yan, Z. (2014). Trust Management in Mobile Cloud Computing. In *Trust Management in Mobile Environments: Autonomic and Usable Models* (pp. 54–93). Hershey, PA: IGI Global. doi:10.4018/978-1-4666-4765-7.ch004

Zardari, M. A., & Jung, L. T. (2016). Classification of File Data Based on Confidentiality in Cloud Computing using K-NN Classifier. *International Journal of Business Analytics*, *3*(2), 61–78. doi:10.4018/IJBAN.2016040104

Zhang, C., Simon, J. C., & Lee, E. (2016). An Empirical Investigation of Decision Making in IT-Related Dilemmas: Impact of Positive and Negative Consequence Information. *Journal of Organizational and End User Computing*, *28*(4), 73–90. doi:10.4018/JOEUC.2016100105

Zou, J., Wang, Y., & Orgun, M. A. (2015). Modeling Accountable Cloud Services Based on Dynamic Logic for Accountability. *International Journal of Web Services Research*, *12*(3), 48–77. doi:10.4018/IJWSR.2015070103

About the Authors

Muhammad Usman has completed his PhD in Computer & Information Sciences from Auckland University of Technology, New Zealand. He is currently an Assistant Professor of Computer Science in the department of Computing at Shaheed Zulfikar Ali Bhutto Institute of Science and Technology, Islamabad, Pakistan. His research interests include Data Mining, Data Warehousing, OLAP, Business Intelligence, and Knowledge discovery. He is currently researching in the novel methods and techniques for the seamless integration of Data Mining and Data Warehousing technologies. He has published in international journals and conference proceedings, and he has served as reviewer for a number of premier journals and conferences.

M. Usman has completed his Masters in Computer Science from ZABIST, Islamabad, Pakistan. He is currently working as Web Manager at Pakistan Scientific and Technological Information Center, Islamabad, Pakistan. His research interests include Data Mining, Data Warehousing and Knowledge discovery. He has published his research work in international journals and conference proceedings.

Index

A

association 9, 17-18, 20-33, 37, 47-49, 52, 59, 61, 65-66, 71-74, 76-78, 81, 96, 99, 101, 103-104, 110, 112, 117-119, 124, 131, 134, 139-140, 142-143, 150
average error rate 35, 42-43, 45

C

classification 9, 16, 34, 41, 50, 52, 60, 78-82, 85-89, 101-104, 106, 108-110, 122-124, 127-131, 140-143, 145-146, 148-150
cluster 4-5, 9, 25-26, 37, 39-41, 49, 52, 62, 64-66, 68, 71-76, 78-80, 82-85, 87, 89, 92-95, 97, 99-108, 110, 112-114, 116-118, 122-129, 131, 134-139, 141-146, 148, 150
Cover Type 131, 133, 135-138, 143, 150

D

data 1-4, 7-10, 14-16, 18-21, 23-31, 33-43, 45-53, 59-62, 64-68, 70-71, 73-74, 76, 78-89, 91-97, 99, 102-103, 106, 108-114, 117, 123-124, 127-131, 133-136, 139-142, 145-146, 148-150
dataset 9-10, 23, 27, 38-40, 45, 47-48, 51, 59, 61-62, 64-65, 68-69, 71, 76, 78, 81, 85, 91, 93-94, 99, 102, 106, 110-113, 116, 118, 127, 131, 133-134, 136-138, 146

E

evaluation 3-4, 9, 14-19, 25-29, 33, 35, 41-45, 48-49, 51, 59-61, 78, 82, 84, 86, 88-89, 102, 104-106, 109-110, 112, 122, 124-125, 128, 130-131, 134, 140, 143, 145-146, 149-150
Extraction 1-5, 7-9, 14-17, 19-20, 33, 35, 37, 45-46, 49, 51-53, 59-61, 72, 78, 85, 89, 91, 97, 100-102, 106, 110-112, 122-123, 127, 131, 133-134, 141-142, 146, 150

F

finding hidden patterns 20, 35
Forest Cover 131, 133, 138, 150

G

generation 4, 9, 18, 20, 25, 27, 37, 39, 43, 49, 52, 59-61, 71, 78, 85, 89, 96, 102, 106, 110, 112, 116, 122, 127, 131, 134, 137, 141, 146, 150

H

hidden interesting patterns 21-23, 35, 49
hierarchical clusters 61, 64, 78, 92, 101-102, 112-113, 121-122, 134-135, 140-141

K

Knowledge 1-3, 5, 8-9, 14-17, 19-23, 26, 33-38, 45, 48-52, 62

M

machine 9, 19, 27-28, 37, 39, 41, 43, 91, 110-111, 131, 133

measures 2-5, 9, 14-19, 21, 26-29, 31-33, 35-36, 41-47, 49-52, 59, 74-77, 80, 82-89, 99-100, 103, 105-110, 117-119, 124-131, 140, 142-143, 145-150

mining 1-5, 9, 14-36, 39-42, 44-52, 59, 61, 66-67, 71, 73, 76, 78, 96, 99, 102, 112, 117-118, 123, 134, 139-141

model 4-5, 9, 21, 23, 36-37, 39-41, 43-45, 47, 50-53, 59-62, 64, 66-68, 71, 73-75, 78, 80-84, 86-87, 89, 91-96, 101-105, 107-114, 116-117, 122, 124-127, 129, 131, 133, 135-137, 139-140, 142-145, 147-150

multidimensional environment 2-3, 15-16, 19, 21, 23, 26-29, 32, 35, 41-42, 51, 87, 108, 129, 147-148

N

nominal variables 9, 22, 25, 37, 39-40, 52, 60-62, 64-65, 67-68, 73, 87, 91, 93-96, 102, 108, 111, 113-116, 123, 129, 133, 135-138, 148

P

Pattern 1-5, 7, 9, 14-17, 19-21, 23, 27-29, 33-36, 39-40, 42-43, 45-46, 49-53, 59-61, 77-78, 82, 85, 87, 89, 91, 97, 100-102, 106-107, 109-112, 121-123, 127, 129, 131, 133-134, 140-142, 146-147, 150

Prediction 1-5, 7-9, 14-17, 34-46, 50-53, 59-60, 67, 77-78, 80, 83-89, 91, 95, 101-111, 114, 121-125, 127-131, 133, 137, 140-143, 145-150

proposed framework 61, 77, 101, 112, 121, 134, 140

R

rules 5, 9, 17-30, 32-33, 37, 48-50, 52, 59, 61, 71-78, 81, 89, 96-101, 103-104, 110, 112, 117-119, 123-124, 131, 134, 139-140, 142-143, 150

S

schema 4, 9, 18-19, 22, 25, 28, 30, 40, 47, 49, 52, 59-61, 68, 70-75, 85, 87, 89, 96-97, 106-108, 110, 112, 116-118, 127-129, 131, 134, 137-140, 145-148, 150

software error 16, 51

T

techniques 1-5, 7, 9, 14-23, 26, 30, 32-42, 45-53, 98

U

UCI 9-10, 19, 27-28, 37, 39, 41, 91, 110-111, 131, 133

V

visualization 2-3, 5, 9, 14-15, 17-19, 30-33, 48, 50, 52, 59, 61, 76-77, 83-84, 89, 99-101, 104-105, 110, 112, 118, 122, 124-126, 131, 134, 142-143, 145, 150

volume 1, 7, 17, 23, 25, 34-35, 37, 41, 51, 134

W

warehouse environment 3-4, 9, 14, 16-18, 29, 33, 35-36, 45, 49, 51, 53, 60, 85, 106, 127, 146, 148

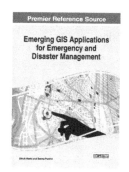
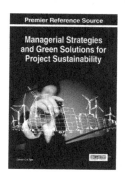

Printed in the United States
By Bookmasters